Eat, Drink & BE WARY

Cautionary tales
by KATHY BIEHL

9TH HOUSE

EAT, DRINK & BE WARY:
CAUTIONARY TALES

© Kathy Biehl 2021.
All Rights Reserved.

FIRST EDITION
First Printing, 2021

ISBN 978-1-7364321-1-2

Book design by Noah Diamond
Cover concept by Matthew Foster
Author photo by Suzanne Savoy

9th House
P.O. Box 184
Oak Ridge, NJ 07438

9thHouse.Biz

Printed in the United States of America

"If you love to eat and have a sense of humor Kathy will have you chuckling at her stories and craving some Doritos. She proves that writing about food doesn't have to be so darn serious. I wish it could all be this fun."

— SUE REDDEL
Food Travelist

"Three cheers (salt, butter, and sugar) for Kathy Biehl's wittily, wonderfully worded collection of mouth watering essays. Reading *Eat, Drink & Be Wary* was like going on a tasting tour — with a menu that encompasses not just food but the deeply felt culture that surrounds it. Culinary primitives like me will also be glad to know that the smorgasbord frequently skirts the exclusive grottoes of gourmetism and makes a beeline towards delicious, delicious junk. Devour this book!"

— TRAV S.D.
author, *No Applause, Just Throw Money:*
The Book That Made Vaudeville Famous and the blog Travalanche

"I love little books like this. They're like going to a coffee house for an hour with a good friend and just spilling the beans. And this one is focused on the major appetite we can talk about in mixed company. A fun, cathartic book we all need to have at hand to cleanse our metaphorical reading palates."

— JOHN-MICHAEL ALBERT
author of 8 volumes of poetry (most recent:
Questions You Were Too Polite to Ask, Marble Kite Press, 2018)
and 8th Poet Laureate of Portsmouth, NH (2011-2013)

Menu

EAT, DRINK & BE WARY

"Food is an important part of a balanced diet."

— FRAN LEBOWITZ

INTRODUCTION

Food and drink do a lot more than address physical need. They play a central role in our emotional and social existence. They serve as currency for hospitality, love, and affection, as a security blanket and plug for psychic wounds, and as a touchstone for times that have slipped into memory. They provide an excuse for people to sit together and share a meal, a round or two, and, often, the experience of connection.

Cognoscenti have long laid claim to this turf. They got a lot of company – and competition – in the late 20th century, when food and drink escalated into the stuff of entertainment, foodie and cocktail cultures, multiple TV networks, and intellectual superiority.

I wandered through this terrain as it morphed, downed a lot of meals and drinks both appalling and delighting, typed up observations for all manner of publications, and usually got paid to do it. I didn't set out to spend decades writing about bars, restaurants, food, and the behaviors they occasion. (My freelance writing focused on offbeat travel and what used to go by human interest.) The topics threw themselves across my path, in the initial years, in a real-world lead-in to an old joke.

A girl walks into a bar and …

It did begin with a bar, or rather, lots of them. A former boyfriend passed on a gig he was leaving, writing short, snappy listings of Houston bars for

Texas Monthly. Actually walking into a bar played a role, too. I was only a few yards into a pub late one evening when a reporter I'd gone out with flagged me over to say that his paper was losing its restaurant reviewer and I had the right style for the job. No, thanks, I said. The resolve lasted until he phoned my office the next day with the *Houston Business Journal*'s editor-in-chief on the line. (One moral of these stories: Don't burn bridges.)

In the 30 years since that call, I have reviewed restaurants for newspapers, magazines, directories, and guides, reported food news for national publications, and written about wine for magazines. My career coincided with Houston's culinary scene rising to national prominence; my base of operations expanded to New York City and, eventually, the entire country. A cultural anthropologist by nature, I picked up great and sometimes incredible stories that fell outside the scope of assignments (and their mainstream frame of reference). Those found venting in my long-running, self-published zine and its companion blogs.

This book consists primarily of magazine and zine articles. When I began compiling the collection, the vignettes and focus and frame of reference struck me as artifacts from a distant era. (Iced coffee an anomaly?!?) As I write this introduction during a pandemic, a thick glass wall is now between me and the world I prowled and captured. It was one in which people gathered at tables and counters, raised glasses, shared food, and engaged in dramas and laughter and magic.

I invite you to join me, from the socially safe distance of reading, press your face against the glass, and peer into a time that was.

KATHY BIEHL
September 2020
Cozy Lake, NJ

*"Food,
my favorite!"*

— Norm

THE CELLULAR
MEMORY OF FOOD

Proust had his madeleines. For me, it's Doritos and Dr Pepper.

Food isn't just about nutrition. Argue all you want that the reason you eat is to fuel your body; if you're reading this, food actually has quite another, larger meaning for you. (Unless, of course, you're my friend who serves himself cornflakes for dinner — the revelation of which neatly cut off the possibility of his ever becoming more than my friend.)

If food were merely the equivalent of gasoline, why do we talk and think and care so much about it? For vast segments of this society, food offers refuge from a cruel, uncaring or, perhaps, merely boring world. Food is a diversion, a hobby, an obsession, a form of entertainment swelling to faddish proportions. Just look at the rise of celebrity chefs, avalanche of high-profile cookbooks, and proliferation of television cooking shows (why, in some parts of the country,[1] there's even a cable channel dedicated to nothing else).

Too, food has a profound connection to the subconscious, particularly the nooks and crannies having to do with Mom and nurturing. What, where, when, why, and how we eat are questions fraught with emotional significance and baggage. Through our choices, we reconnect with something more than

---

[1] When this piece was published, Houston's cable company had dropped The Food Network.

whatever's going on at the moment. Some of us seek to recapture sensations we enjoyed at the family table or elsewhere in the past, which is part of the driving force behind holiday traditions and rituals. Others of us are looking instead to compensate for a childhood of lousy meals.

I think about this subject a lot, and I'm finding that food also guards a weird intersection point between the subconscious and our bodies. I stumbled upon the correlation during a bout of therapy a few years back. My therapist suggested I try talking to my inner child by writing down questions and seeing what answers bubbled up. I dutifully wrote, "What do you want?" and was startled to watch my hand scrawl out demands that my conscious mind would not have generated. Second on the list was "an Almond Joy."

Now, if you'd asked me moments earlier what my favorite candy bars were when I was a kid, this is not what I would have answered. Snickers and Heath Bar would have been on the list, but not Almond Joy. Not only was it not a favorite, but I don't even have strong memories of eating one.

When my therapist heard the list of demands, he suggested devising a meal entirely for my inner child. And so I found myself wandering through Kroger making mismatched impulse purchases with a nutritionally unsound cumulative impact: Klondike bars, iced raisin cookies and, yes, an Almond Joy for the four-year-old (the inner me was screaming for attention at a variety of ages, it seemed); Doritos and Dr Pepper for the preteen me.

The appeal of those particular cookies and the candy bar was a mystery, but I knew the reasons for the bookend items. Klondikes were the only treat I can remember having, except for birthday cake, before second grade. Doritos and Dr Pepper were my absolute favorite snack food in late elementary school and junior high. I only got to have the combination at my best friend's slumber parties; since I never had the combination at home (and was rarely allowed either component alone), they smacked of indulgence that was otherwise denied. The memory is still so complex and gripping that typing this out is bringing to mind the plush, dark green carpet of my pal's room, where we laid out our bedrolls, snacked and giggled and listened to records and, eventually, fell asleep.

The peculiar meal (yes, disgusting as it sounds, I sampled everything at one sitting) worked the desired effect. My subconscious began calming down with this tangible proof that it could really have what it wanted. Transformation wasn't immediate, of course, but the food-laden signal was the beginning of the process.

Deliberately summoning a food memory is tricky. Either a connection occurs or it doesn't; you can't force the effect, regardless of how badly you want it. My mother used to tackle an Easter bread recipe that she associated with her Czech grandmother. The attempts always fell short. No matter how carefully she followed the instructions or how much she kneaded the dough, the bread never had the taste she remembered — and the process failed to conjure up her grandmother's bustling, relative-filled kitchen, which I suspect was the true aim.

When a memory bubbles up without forewarning or intentional prodding, though, that's when the magic occurs. Sometimes the memory's so deep that it's difficult to attach language to it; sometimes it simply resonates in your cells. However the memory surfaces — in your psyche or your body; whether the recognition is instantaneous or slow to form — the result is the same: It plugs you into a distant spot on the time/space continuum and you wobble momentarily, at least internally, as you figure out where you are.

The clearest, least disorienting experience occurs with the sight of once-familiar food. Towards the end of the summer college program I attended in Austria, a carton of Pepperidge Farm Goldfish crackers turned up at a party. Their presence set off an epidemic of homesickness, even in those of us who'd been boycotting student-led expeditions to McDonald's. Up to that moment we'd acclimated ourselves to daily life enough for it to no longer feel foreign. The illusion of feeling at home collapsed in an instant at the appearance of something strangely beloved from Home. Fortunately, any anguish was short-lived (as were the Goldfish); I recall my coterie comforting ourselves generously with an enormous punch bowl filled with white wine and berries.

My brother had a less pleasant landing when a dinner invitation from me shot him back to a place he never wanted to revisit. About a decade ago I took him to what had been the Romana Cafeteria on Buffalo Speedway, where I'd been having consistently and surprisingly good meals. I had no idea until we drove up that its name had changed. When my brother saw Luby's on the sign, he emphatically refused to get out of the car. Every part of his being bolted at the specter of childhood visits to the neighborhood Luby's (the one with Miss Inez at the organ, across from SMU in Dallas). Our eyes were invariably bigger than our stomachs, a disparity with unfortunate and painful consequences, since our parents did not allow us to waste anything we'd taken. So what if it had been a decade since he'd staggered out of Luby's? The memories retained a tyrannical hold. We went to Niko Niko's.

My friends David and Rex have been living in a kind of laboratory for cellular food memories, a lab that spills out from their shared kitchen into the outside world. David once saw Rex put powdered milk into their grocery cart, to make sure that they always have milk on hand (they've increased their cooking at home in the last year or so). While Rex continued down the aisle, David shot back to the kitchen of his early childhood, where his mother was reconstituting powdered milk in large plastic jugs. His father bought 50 lb. containers of powdered milk not because he was poor, but because he was cheap, David recalls. The memory caused no lingering damage; my friend is coexisting with boxed milk now with no ill effect.

On another trip to the store, the tables turned. Rex caught sight of pinto beans and was visited by his mother producing big pots of them, with homemade chow chow on the side. He suggested to David that they make some, then the conversation turned to people who do and people who don't put ketchup on pinto beans.

David's buttering a bowl of steamed white rice (in their kitchen, for a change) prompted the knee-jerk remark "You're making breakfast food" from Rex. In his childhood home, he had to explain, rice with milk, sugar, and a couple of slices of ripped up bread sometimes served as cereal substitute. Another one was milk toast, two slices sprinkled with sugar and sliced into thirds, horizontally and vertically, the middle one saved for last because it was the squishiest. Anytime he runs across a dish that his mother used as nutrition on a shoestring, like the rice, pinto beans, or milk toast, he has a split reaction: on the one hand, it's po' folk food; on the other, nothing is so comforting. "Conscious me has become gentrified," he confesses, adding "I didn't mean it, and it's only on an academic level." "Subconscious me," he confesses, "is still true to the universe."

The experiences of my brother, David, and Rex point to an inherent power of food that fascinates me: the momentary recapturing of earlier time on which the door is normally bolted. Suddenly you recall: This is how I used to feel; this is how life was. These time-travel moments are rare and elusive. Modern American society offers little opportunity for distance; the cultural trappings of the past surround us still, with television and radio providing easy, almost unavoidable access to the programs and music of the previous four or five decades, and chain restaurants have homogenized dietary preferences

across the country. When we do manage to lurch backwards, it's so uncommon that it's mesmerizing.

More often than sight, I've found, taste (which, of course, works hand-in-hand with smell) is the key that unlocks the doors of memory. Some part of your being, perhaps your psyche, perhaps the very cells of your body, recognizes a stimulus as familiar, and then your brain scrambles to figure out why. It's as if tiny beings flip switches on a control board, with each flip shooting a memory onto an enormous monitor until one feels right and locks into place. This one? No. This one? Close. This one? Bingo.

A vanilla-flavored meringue cookie sent my boyfriend on a "What *is* this?" quest. He knew he'd had the taste before; he knew it stemmed from childhood, but it took nibble after nibble before he erupted with the answer: the marshmallows in Lucky Charms. As soon as he put a name to it, I could taste it, too.

Childhood treats loom large in food memories. They resurrect times when our jobs consisted of being a kid and someone else worried about where our food was coming from and who was going to pay for it. And within this category, the most universally potent of treats is old-fashioned candy. Mention the subject to any Baby Boomer and you will unleash recollections of haunting candy counters after school and lustily eyeing (and sometimes buying) goodies that no longer fill the shelves of today.

Thoughts like that filled my mind as I did some sleuthing for a magazine article on sources for old-fashioned candy. The owner of one company that's since shuttered told me she couldn't look at a box of Lemonheads without thinking of getting in trouble for sneaking them into class 30 years ago (and remembering that the teacher's scolding didn't make her quit; it just made her chew more quietly).

In this research process, my first strong reaction was to Nik-L-Nips, a five-pack of wax bottles filled with day-glo liquids. They took me back to after school visits to M.E. Moses, where a black-haired, middle-aged cashier kept watch while I circled around and around displays crowded with Slo-Pokes, Sugar Daddies, pastel-colored sugar bead bracelets, and other delights. My tolerance for sugar no longer being what it was, the adult in me overrode any inner-child impulse to bite open one of the wax bottles. Still, respecting their nostalgic potential, I bought a case for a friend's 40th birthday party. The people who took the bait (a surprisingly numerous lot) confirmed that the contents were sickeningly sweet water.

The research catapulted me into a sensurround experience at Economy Candy, a 65-year-old wonderland in the remaining Jewish enclave of Manhattan's Lower East Side. I stepped into a maze of industrial shelving, rising higher than any human's reach and blanketed with enormous plastic bags of lollipops and candy bars. Below the front counter stretched an expanse of haphazardly stacked, opened cardboard boxes teeming with wax lips, Pop Rocks, white drawstring bags of bubble gum "gold," rainbow-colored conical pops, and other long-lost objects of desire. Even more lined the back wall, which was a veritable altar of candies by the pound in gigantic glass jars. It was M.E. Moses to the tenth power. If I'd been a grade schooler, I probably would have thrown up from excitement. Even as an adult, I was feeling pretty woozy. It didn't help that the sound system was blasting Louis Prima whipping up a frenzy. (Want to take your inner child on a shopping spree? Surf to economycandy.com.)

For those of us who've lived in now-distant places, food can deliver a ticket back to our previous homes. I once knew a Vietnamese man who could not endure a day without rice. If he'd made it till evening without any, he would come home after a restaurant dinner, spoon a bowl of rice out of refrigerator leftovers, and eat it standing in the kitchen until his psyche was fed.

The association can be purely personal, too. Malted milk brings back island life to a friend who spent his first decade on Aruba and Puerto Rico. The taste reminds him of a packaged drink called Great Shakes, which was a favorite of his when he lived in Puerto Rico, and which required an elaborate ritual of mixing the contents of a triangular flavor packet into the container that came with the drink.

What sends me traveling is authentic food from Germany and Austria. I spent ninth grade in Munich and lived for a summer in Austria five years later, and haven't visited either country since — at least, not physically. A few incidents, though, have transported me back there astrally.

The first occurred at the end of a driveway off a two-lane road in New Ulm, Texas. I was following signs to Hackemack's Hofbräuhaus, which I'd seen advertised on an aging billboard. As soon as I drove up, the very cells in my body leapt at the sight of steep-pitched gables, antlers under the peak, window boxes with heart cut-outs, and wooden patio tables sporting Spatenbräu umbrellas. My body knew before my mind did that this exterior was straight from Bavaria.

The food didn't have the same impact on me when I made a return trek for dinner, but, to be fair, few German restaurants in this country have. In the last two years, though, I've come across two that ambushed me with familiarity. The Silver Swan in Manhattan delivered exquisitely authentic *Weisswurst* that took me back to my last day in Munich, when my favorite classmate and I picked plump white veal sausages out of a steaming, parsley-filled pot at a dignified restaurant near the royal residence. Even the mustard struck me as a long-lost friend; instead of a crock, it came in a tube, which brought to

mind another classmate's kitchen, where we'd shared after-school sandwiches.

A Queens restaurant called Zum Stammtisch sent me into intoxication before even ordering, and not just from the stein of dark beer I was draining. It was a minefield of detonating memories, set off by hearing a gang of old guys arguing in German at the bar and then recognizing one, then another and, gradually, every single painting in the dining room where we were seated. Before swallowing the first bite of the *Leberkäs* (like liverwurst, except in big fat slices and pan-fried), I was 19 years old again, sitting in a cramped corner of Donisl, an ancient eatery in the center of Munich.

Restaurants occupy a special place in the distance-spanning category of food memories. Call it restaurant row on memory lane, if you like. Who among us has not returned to a former hometown without even a short list of restaurants you wanted to visit? I'm certainly not immune.

For years, food pilgrimages straitjacketed my trips back to Austin, where I attended law school. My route had not only required stops, but required dishes at each one: at Casita Jorges, beef enchiladas; at Mad Dog and Beans, a quarter-pounder and Bluebell peppermint ice cream shake. The mecca of all meccas was Milto's Pizza Pub, which turned out the best souvlaki sandwiches I've ever had (and I keep looking). I valued Milto's as a personal stage as well. Each visit stirred scenes from the halcyon days of studying for the bar, before the working world crashed in on me. It was there I walked in on two natural food store owners genially fixing prices over a pitcher of beer, and there the most spectacular drinking binge of my life culminated in a Baptist preacher's son recognizing me as a fellow Highland Park High School graduate.

The tenacity of my attraction to Milto's underscored the true nature of my quest. With each stop on my restaurant tour, there was no question that the food was outstanding. It was not the goal, though, but a route to it. The real pilgrimage was to the past. Jonathan Richman hits on this in a song called "Summer Feeling," in which he rhapsodizes about an ancient crush and asks "Do you long for her or the way you were?" The way we were, definitely. It's not the food I was after. It was who I used to be.

There's a theory — it might be scientific fact, for all I know — that radio and television waves are bounding around the universe, so that an alien civilization's receiver could intercept and replay them. Food memories, I think, hold a similar possibility. Through them we pick up broadcasts from the past, like fragments of an ancient or erratic transmission. We can't always tune them in deliberately, but every so often, they appear spontaneously. And as we stop what we're doing to take them in, we step, momentarily, outside linear time.

My Table, 2001

"*Laughter is brightest in the place where the food is.*"

— IRISH PROVERB

EATING OUT IS FUN!
HOUSTON, ITALIAN STYLE

Tutto Bene!, just north of the High School for Performing Cops in the lovely lower Houston Heights, where curbs have yet to separate the yards from the streets, has quickly proven itself an endearing bastion of eccentricity. The evidence:

Visit the first: Friday dinner. A round table draped with red cloth, topped with a Chianti bottle-cum-candleholder and standing next to the trailer advertising sign at the street's edge gave the first impression, which held the great promise of weirdness. My first encounter with the staff took the theme and ran with it. "Smoking or non-smoking?" the hostess asked. Before I could answer, a lanky man bolted from the dining room and interrupted. "Or would you prefer indoors or outdoors?" "Outdoors? We don't serve outdoors," the hostess protested. "We do now; I served out there at lunch. I'll show you," he said, taking off down a corridor alongside the bar. She followed, and my party did, too. Through a window, a table – one lone table – was in fact visible, set up on a small deck in the middle of the backyard. We declined and took a seat in non-smoking, not far from a small framed box of about 13 different types of pasta, labeled. (Rex thought them much like the barbed wire displays proudly mounted in every freeway diner on I-20.)

While we contemplated the menu, the same lanky man (who was beginning to look a lot like the owner) dropped by cradling a bottle of white wine and encouraging us to order one because his distributor talked him into buying a case of it. He was followed by a waitress who began her explanation of the blackboard menu with an unforgettable question: "You're probably wondering: what's the difference between shrimp capri and shrimp uncapri?"

Visit two: Lunchtime. The owner, wearing shorts, was standing on the sidewalk and sipping from a huge cup of iced tea. "I'm still pushing outdoors," he said as we walked inside. Near the end of the meal, he appeared tableside. My companion asked about the pesto's ingredients; it was so mild (but delicious) that he was sure spinach was included. "I'm horrified!" the owner declaimed, spreading his hand across his chest. Mild, it turns out, is the exact opposite of what he's shooting for. He even grows the basil in his own garden to get a large enough amount, since his menu price turned out to be too low to cover the herb's market cost.

Visit three: The music was full of gooey romantic ballads that my mother hadn't heard in years. No Sinatra; no Bennett – even more saccharine than them.

Visit four: The office party. When the owner spotted us, I told him that earlier in the week I'd brought my parents, so now I was bringing my office. He bent down, kissed my right hand, and promised to kiss the other one when I brought my whole block. He later sighted us with his pepper grinder. The Parmesan grinder, he explained, was the only Italian piece of machinery that he believes works – and he can say that because he lived in Italy! But not only that, he had a Fiat for a while with no end of engine problems that he described in forgettable detail. At the end of the meal, he approached us with a giant, still supple fish draped over (and extending about a foot from either side of) his out-stretched arms. "Know anyone you want to send this to?" he asked us. Most of the table recoiled. "What *is* that?" someone demanded. "It's a redfish," he answered. "A very unhappy redfish." It was that night's special, and he said we had to come back to eat it. He later told me that the chef had a sick sense of humor (imagine) and was planning to cut off its head, put a cigar in its mouth, and stick it in a bucket of ice.

Ladies' Fetish & Taboo Society
Compendium of Urban Anthropology, 1990

"Best Bird Ever!"

Part of the appeal of a road trip is scouting out new food experiences. One that proved worth the drive topped off a recent visit to the National Baseball Hall of Fame in Cooperstown, NY (a museum which, by the way, has great merit for the cultural history it engrossingly lays out, for those of us who aren't particularly fans of the sport). My boyfriend had been on alert about a semi-nearby barbecue joint ever since seeing it featured in an episode of the Food Network show "$40 a Day." Our party followed his urging and detoured some 40 minutes to Brooks' House of Bar-B-Que on Oneonta, where a neon animation of a hatchet-wielding cook chasing a chicken signaled our arrival. The omens were favorable.

Brooks, a nearly 45-year-old restaurant that evolved from a poultry farm, was built to serve the masses. It boasts a seating capacity of 300, as well as the largest indoor charcoal pit in the Northeast. Despite an enormous, well-populated parking lot and a switchback line at the dining room door, the wait for a table was short-lived. It wasn't even 30 minutes before we were in sight of rooster-patterned wallpaper within, a mid-20th-century mural of the egg-to-platter life cycle of a chicken, and framed mementos from "$40 a Day" host Rachael Ray's visit, including a menu inscribed "Best Bird Ever!" (in handwriting as extroverted as her TV personality).

The chicken is good. In fact, it was far and away the tastiest and most tender of the bar-b-que samplers that swamped my table. Brooks' bar-b-que sauce, which it sells online and by mail order, is of the smoky, somewhat sweet variety, and the kitchen adds eggs to the marinade for the chicken.

What most grabbed my attention, though, was our friendly speed demon of a waiter. He was depositing the drink orders before my party returned from the salad bar. "You're on top of things!" I exclaimed. "You have to be," he laughed.

He later provided the capping moment of the experience. As we were littering the table with crumpled, soiled napkins, he leaned toward the other woman in our party.

"You said you wanted strawberries with your cheesecake, didn't you?"

"Oh, I don't have room for dessert," she protested.

He looked at me and smiled. "Carrot cake for you?"

"Oh, I wish!" I sighed.

"I can make wishes come true, ma'am," he countered. "I'm the dessert genie!"

LLRX.com, 2005

"There ain't no such thing as wrong food."

— SEAN STEWART

THE JOY OF JUNK FOOD
NUTRITION HAS NOTHING TO DO WITH IT

(juŋk´ fōod) *n.* A combination of fat, salt, and/or sugar that goes against the dictates of nutrition, better judgment, or common sense.

Admit it: You like it. It may not be in your pantry. It may not even be in your normal diet. But it's in your life. It's under your skin. And more often than you'd probably admit, it's in your mouth.

It's the dirty little secret of the food world. We're all susceptible. It's only human. No matter how sophisticated our sensibilities may be, no matter how devoutly we embrace locally raised produce and meats, varietal chocolates, estate-bottled olive oils, and whatever rarefied trend may be rounding the culinary bend, each of us has a soft spot for something that we know we really shouldn't eat, but we do anyway. Gleefully.

And that's the nature of junk food. Not to mention its appeal. And reason for existence.

We eat most food because our bodies need something from it. We eat junk because we want it. Forget nutrition — it's not merely beside the point; it's rarely anywhere near the same universe as the point. And what would that be? Indulging in pure physical pleasure, devouring something that tastes soooo good and usually feels good, too. And often, indulging in more than a hint of rebellion as well. Mostly likely someone, somewhere told us not to, and so of course we're attracted. When a single bite can hold the promise of hedonism and defiance, is it any wonder we're hooked?

Don't call this snack food. True, some snacks are junk, and vice versa. But "snack" is too polite for the likes of junk. "Snack" smacks of serving bowls and high-budget advertising campaigns and leaves the door open to edibles with actual nutritional content, like raisins or carrots. It misses out entirely on the potential for messiness and sleaziness and furtiveness and outright slumming inherent in junk food.

Junk food is a luxury. It makes the statement, however unconscious, that we are sufficiently well-off to eat solely out of desire. It is a treat. For a lot of us, junk is a break from the daily diet; for most of us, it's something our childhood caretakers doled out sparingly or on special occasions. Sure, that was for our own good, but the tactic sent a message that has elevated junk food to hallowed status in many a psyche. Soft drinks were so rare an indulgence in the spartan upbringing of one of my friends from childhood that they still inspire reverence in him, despite the rarefied dining he has enjoyed for decades as an international investment banker based in Europe. They sealed his devotion at the age of 10 at most, during his first flight by himself, from Brownsville to Dallas, when he got to have all the Dr Pepper and Coke he could drink. He remembers this thrill better, or so he says, than the free-flowing caviar

JUNK FOOD TIMELINE [2]

Popcorn — 3600 BC

Marshmallows — 2000 BC

Pretzels — bet. 400–610 AD

Soda water — 1767

and champagne on Swissair dayflights from Libreville to whichever European capital was his home at the time.

Being so special, junk food is a reward as well, a use we also learned from our early gatekeepers, who would shake their heads at the sometimes counterproductive ramifications. Another friend (who, incidentally, claims to go to McDonald's for the salads) admits to crowning a several-mile jog, in his younger days, with an entire pint of Baskin & Robbins butter pecan. In the ice cream parlor. Routinely.

Junk food is naughty. It's the bad boy with the motorcycle, the girl whose popularity is the very reason you can't bring her home to meet your family. It's what you're not supposed to eat before dinner or it'll ruin your appetite, or maybe not ever eat at all. Junk food is where we get to break the rules, even the ones we've made for ourselves, and especially the ones we got from our parents.

Junk food is fun, too, and not merely for giving a little rein to our inner adolescent. It's casual party fare, commonplace to the point of being inescapable with all manner of recreation, from going to the movies, an amusement park or a street fair to watching a game on TV with pals. So the sight of it signals: good times ahead.

Most of all, it's fun to eat. Junk food strips refinement and manners from eating and delivers a primal experience. With few exceptions, junk requires you to pick it up and eat it with your fingers. When it drips or oozes, as do

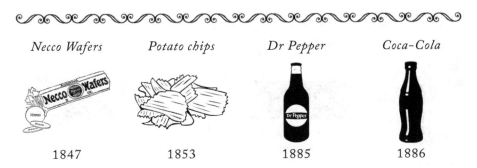

Necco Wafers	Potato chips	Dr Pepper	Coca-Cola
1847	1853	1885	1886

melting ice cream cones or creme-filled doughnuts, that's a cue to catch the escapee in mid-air. If you fail, no problem; there'll be residue to be licked up once the main event is over. This virtue seared Hardee's bacon cheeseburger in one memory, thanks to the salty grease that had to (had to!) be slurped off the paper wrapper.

The most satisfying junk food is highly physical fare. It cracks. It crunches. It squishes. When it resists your bite and then shatters, it supplies immediate stress relief. The next time an unpleasantness ambushes you, try a couple of minutes of explosive crunching and see if you don't agree. And when multiple textures unfold in one bite, that's junk food nirvana, as far as I'm concerned. Peanut M&Ms do the trick for me (unless they're stale; soft peanuts sabotage the effect). If they don't for you, or even if they do, think of what it feels like to bite into a crisp corn chip dripping with soft, creamy dip. Or into French fries, fresh from the fryer, when they have a slightly hardened exterior that cracks to expose a soft, steaming core.

And it's tasty, too. Junk food has a knack for larger-than-life entrances. It clobbers the tongue with exaggerated flavors and seasonings – consider the borderline-painful zing of Hint of Lime Tostitos, Flamin' Hot Limon Cheetos and Atomic Fireballs, the tang of Sweetarts and dill-flavored potato chips, the hyper-sweetness of Mr. Goodbar and Jelly Bellies. The more discomfort the flavorings trigger, they more they linger on after the last morsel has been downed and, in that lingering, awaken the desire for more.

Pepsi-Cola	Hershey bar	Hershey's Kisses	Oreos
1898	1900	1907	1912

And therein lies one of the inherent dangers of junk food. Free will? Ha. Frito-Lay got it right with "Bet you can't eat just one." The slogan was meant for Lay's Potato Chips, but it applies to any type of junk. Junk food overrides the brain. It ignites a repetitive hand-to-mouth motion that hypnotizes the victim into automatic consumption. *I'll just have a couple*, you think, and the interplay of textures and tastes is over so soon that you pop in a few more, and when your eyes come back into focus, probably when you become aware of just how badly you crave a big gulp of some refreshing liquid, half the container or worse has disappeared, along with a small portion of your self-respect. I once sublet an apartment from someone who had the tensile strength of will to leave behind an intact pint of coffee Häagen Dazs, which was on all counts (item, flavor, and brand) an indulgence that I had not previously permitted myself. I stuck a spoon in it at the start of a favorite sitcom and long before the credits rolled – well, let's just say I don't judge my jogger friend.

Once a craving kicks in, there's no telling what a person might do for a fix. I once detoured for a large order of Rally's Cajun fries while en route to dinner at a restaurant I was reviewing. At the time it was a brazen, giddily empowering declaration of autonomy, a variation on a friend's post-college realization that being a grown-up means you can stay up late and eat ice cream any time you want. I now recall an earlier, and singular, precedent in adolescence, when my usually strict mother had driven me through a McDonald's for a large order of fries (during the beef tallow days), pulled into a parking space for us to share

Moon Pies	Eskimo Pie, Marshmallow Fluff	Peter Paul Mounds	Mr. Goodbar
1917	1920	1921	1925

the packet, and then driven through for a second batch.

Weak spots are highly personal. Some people are partial to combinations of salt and fats. Other people prefer their fats with sugars (doughnuts), or their sugars alone (Jolly Ranchers, jawbreakers, even cotton candy, which I actually observed my peers voluntarily consuming at a bar mitzvah party in recent memory). And some of us are omnivores, who have room in our affections for both salty and sweet, apart, alternatingly or all-in-one. (Chocolate-covered potato chips, caramelized nuts, caramel-coated popcorn...heaven.)

Taxonomies can be as idiosyncratic as our preferences. Junk food consists of potato chips but not pretzels, says one friend, Slim Jims but not string cheese, French fries but not hash browns – and never, ever chocolate, even in M&M form. Another omnivore considers deep frying alone to qualify (in his thinking, elevate) any food for junk status. The thought is new to me, but not the love he voices for the crunch, the moist, salty, fatty delicious rush of deep-fried foods.

Kool-Aid	Twinkies	Fritos	Hawaiian Punch
1927	1930	1932	1934

Can any dish in a sit-down restaurant qualify as junk? I hadn't thought in those terms until encountering Bennigan's broccoli bites, which thoroughly disguise the base veggie in a deep fried batter and some manner of hyper-sweetened creaminess and thereby render the broccoli's innate wholesomeness completely moot. So, yes.

Fast food is junk, too. Case closed without argument. Nothing that remains intact a decade after it comes off the grill can be real food, as did the Burger King and McDonald's burgers that a man by the name of Matt Malmgren started collecting in 1992 after finding a perfectly edible-looking cheeseburger and realizing he'd misplaced it a year earlier. (Details are in *Don't Eat This Book* by Morgan Spurlock, whose film *Super Size Me* tracks 30 days he spent eating only at McDonald's.)

What about beverages? Soft drinks are junk, hands down. In my book, so are Kool-Aid, fruit drinks with high-fructose corn syrup, and pretty much every mixed drink that comes with a paper umbrella and/or hasn't seen the light of happy hour since the 1970s (Mai Tais, Singapore slings, sloe gin fizz). Not lite American beer, though. There's junk, and then there's trash.

Some junk foods are regional. The South has MoonPies, weirdly dry graham cookies rendered just as weirdly palatable by a marshmallow filling, super-sweet coating (chocolate or banana is best), and the time-honored tradition of pairing it with R.C. Cola. Texas's bounty runs from heaven-sent Blue Bell Ice Cream to Twang, a sour and salty beer chaser that lurks in small

Krispy Kreme	*York Peppermint Pattie*	*M&Ms*	*Marshmallow Peeps*
1937	1940	1941	1953

packets by cash registers in convenience stores. The state is also blessed by decent distribution of a jewel among junk from Louisiana, Zapp's Spicy Cajun Crawtator Potato Chips. I have seen a frenzy erupt at the mere sight of the red-and-silver-striped bag they come in. Their recreating the slow, feisty burn of a crawfish boil has something to do with it – but so does a love of the culture and the patch of earth that spawned them.

I have observed a similar devotion in the Northeast to the egg cream, a drink that contains neither egg nor cream but instead seltzer water, milk, and chocolate syrup, preferably Fox's U-Bet; Drake's Devil Dogs, dry logs of devil's food cakes that have the primary purpose of encouraging milk consumption, but evoke rhapsodies all the same from people who grew up on them; and Marshmallow Fluff, which has the flavor and whipped texture the name implies, and mystical status as a sandwich companion to peanut butter.

The Midwest and some points north are home to White Castle, a chain revered for tiny square burgers, called "Sliders," with pungent fried onions, steamed buns, and American cheese, if you want it, and meant to be eaten three to six at a time. They are the epitome of sleaze and therefore worthy of great devotion, which the chain has acknowledged by replacing paper take-out bags with cartons labeled "Crave packages." Ordering slyders through bulletproof glass, as I did when I lived in Queens, only enhances the experience. (You should lower expectations for the White Castle packages in the grocery freezer case. They're ... sanitized.)

Chex Mix	*Little Debbie Snack Cake*	*Doritos*	*Pringles*
1954	1960	1966	1971

Question junk preferences at your own risk. Allegiances have deep roots that leave the land of reason behind. You might cringe at the offer of Ruffles and spreadable cream cheese; I once knew an uncle and nephew for whom it spelled ecstasy. The sharing was a private ritual, less scrutable perhaps, but no less compelling to the participants than

heading to Mrs. Johnson's Bakery late at night for doughnuts hot off the line, buying a pint of milk, and finishing both before returning home. That one's in the closet of many a former University of Texas student, mine included.

Alas, junk food does have a dark side. The very things that make it appealing – the fat, the sodium, the sweeteners -- also make it bad for us if we eat much, which we do. (Each year we buy some six million dollars' worth of potato chips and devour upwards of 1.6 billion gallons of ice cream and frozen desserts, enough for 21.5 quarts per person.) There are other consequences beyond what it does to our bodies. It has a profound socio-economic impact on our agricultural base, our workforce, and the food choices available to us, through large-scale processing of cows, chickens, and potatoes, breakneck working conditions, meager wages, and the proliferation of junk food in schools. Look too closely and certain types of junk vaporize into a philosophical battleground. I haven't been able to go near fast food since reading Spurlock's book (the one that mentions the indestructible food collection) and *Fast Food Nation* by Eric Schlosser.

I'm not turning my back on junk food, though, and see little evidence of that in others, either. I still polish off Samoa Girl Scout Cookies with a dispatch that should be shameful. My expat friend comes to this country every summer with a checklist of foods of which he is deprived and therefore must eat, heavy on the junk. Months away from his pilgrimage, he notes in e-mail that he cannot find Twinkies in Great Britain — a continent where Mars Bars are deep fried, for crying out loud, which some might see as a consolation prize.

We won't give up our junk food. After all, we don't eat it for our bodies, but for something more intangible. Which makes it soul food, in a sense. In a certain original recipe, deep-fried, sugar-coated, chocolate-dipped, finger-lickin' good sense.

My Table, 2006

---

² *Sources:* FoodTimeline.org, CandyUSA.com, Hersheys.com, MoonPie.com, The Coca-Cola Company, National Museum of American History Archives, MarshmallowFluff.com, Adams County Historical Society, Frito-Lay, Dr Pepper/7up, Inc. (now the Dr Pepper Snapple Group), Krispy Kreme, Pepsi-Cola, Wikipedia

CALLING THE SPREAD
TALK ABOUT MAYO? HOW COULD I RESIST?

A middle-aged woman with a clipboard halted me outside Marshall Field's in the Galleria. She asked if I'd answer questions about food and assured me earnestly that it wouldn't require any tasting.

Something about my appearance says: stop this woman and ask her questions. I can cut off survey-takers without a second thought when they call me at home, but let them approach me in person and inexplicably politeness takes over. This apparently undisguisable personality defect has singled me out to an annoying range of people who make a point of piercing my anonymity, including street performers and state-fair auto demonstrators.

Talking to this woman seemed low-risk enough. She looked like a school teacher or someone's kindly aunt, and I have made a habit out of talking to people about food. Besides, shopping had triggered a contemplation of certain corporeal developments, not entirely unrelated to the proposed topic, that was fast spiraling toward depression. Answering a few questions could only be a welcome diversion.

She rattled off questions and noted responses on a sheet already littered with pencil markings. What age group did I fall in? The answer was one I didn't mind owning up to. Had I participated in a market research survey in the last six months? Nope; been steering clear of malls lately.

She eliminated a bevy of food industry conglomerates as my employer and reached the heart quickly: "In the last six months have you eaten mustard? Ketchup? Mayonnaise? Margarine?" I said yes to the middle two. She lit up.

"What brands of mayonnaise?" Homemade, I answered. This stumped her. I made it myself, I explained. Her form had no spot for that response.

"No product mayonnaise?"

"Safflower mayonnaise," I said. Her brow wrinkled. Would I repeat that? Sure. Her form had no spot for that response, either. I was starting to enjoy this. Skewing statistical bases is one of life's great pleasures.

The earnest look returned. I would have been happy to stand there for another ten minutes or so, giving, explaining, and spelling answers for which her form had no space, but she was obviously ready to move this interview to another level.

"Would you participate in a mayonnaise review?" she asked. "It'll take two minutes and I promise" – she intensified her gaze – "I'm telling the truth." She intoned the last three words as if conveying a coded message.

This was an offer no self-respecting magnet for weird could pass up. She took me down a hallway I'd never noticed in a decade of stomping through the Galleria; the commercial counterpart of Brigadoon, perhaps? A sign jutted into the hallway with the name of a market research firm.

She opened a door and welcomed me into an office as if we had just been introduced. A young man stood up behind a desk and greeted me as well. He smiled at her knowingly. The scene had the vague air of an unfilmed Monty Python sketch.

She ushered me down another hallway to a room with four tables separated by dividers. A man about my age was seriously filling out a pamphlet questionnaire. My table had a bunch of detergent containers barely disguised by a sheet of blue plastic. The woman excused herself, this time promising to be gone for two seconds.

Off on the time by a factor of about 100, she returned with a blue cafeteria tray covered by a leaf of foil. Under the foil was a pair of plates, each with a spoon protruding from a congealed blob of mayonnaise large enough to grease down white-bread-and-cold-cut sandwiches for a family of six.

Not only do I not have any particular aversion to mayonnaise, I actually kind of like the stuff, unlike a friend who recoils at even the sound of its name. This double-dosed spectacle would have pushed her phobia past evasion tactics and rendered her unable to walk a grocery-store condiment aisle ever again. It certainly sobered me.

No question here of transgressing the survey's ground rules and sneaking a taste. One sample had a stringently homogenized smoothness, benign save for the magnitude of the serving, while its companion, discolored and bumpy, was downright nasty-looking.

The researcher opened a questionnaire and began the interrogation.

"Which is more lumpy, the one on the left or the one on the right?" Seeing as how one had a complete absence of lumps and the other had virtually nothing but them, the answer was indisputable: the right.

"Which is more yellow, the one on the left or the one on the right?" Again, no reasonable minds could differ: the right.

She scribbled these responses on paper and took my name and phone number. I waited for the next question. She asked me instead to sign a verification that I had in fact given my opinion about the mayonnaise samples. I grinned widely.

"Please don't smile," she chastised. "You'd be surprised how hard it is to get someone to do this right."

She ushered me back through the reception area. The young man again rose from his desk, offered thanks, and bid me goodbye. I returned, laughing, to the mall as I had known it.

The experience had irrevocably altered my frame of reference, though. I was now aware of clip-board clutching individuals standing before me in every direction. I was still chuckling when a researcher loomed near the elevator bank. As I successfully escaped his attention, a fleeting thought disturbed my amusement:

What if I'd said yes to mustard?

Houston Press, 1991

"*If you are ever at a loss to support a flagging conversation, introduce the subject of eating.*"

— Leigh Hunt

FOOD GAMES
I WAS A GAME SHOW CONTESTANT (ALMOST)

All I wanted was a seat in the audience of a Food Network game show. I got one, all right, with a backstage pass, to boot.

It began with passing time on the subway by scanning the classifieds on the back of the *New York Press*. Amidst the usual thanks to St. Jude and calls for medical studies, I spied a request for contestants and audience members for a new Food Network game show.

This seemed rife with potential for a self-taught urban anthropologist. I love watching the off-screen goings-on at TV tapings, and this one held the promise of great amusement, perverse and otherwise. The Food Network was responsible for the worst game show I've ever seen, *Pressure Cooker*, which combined a byzantine quiz format with a 60-second race to make celebrity portraits out of food. Nadir: immortalizing Whoopi Goldberg with a watermelon. This actually aired.

Whatever this new creation was, I had to see it.

A hurdle to my goal soon presented itself. I'd have to test to be a contestant. This requirement sent me to a plain room behind an unmarked door in the upper 50s near the Hudson River, where I spent more than an hour communing with a surprisingly varied slice of human life. Only after some 50 of us filled out sheets of personal questions (Any allergies? Anything you will not eat? You bet: tripe. Once is enough) did we get an explanation of what was going on.

An athletic, hyper-upbeat young man named Brent explained that we were testing for a revamping of *Pressure Cooker*. Its name was *Taste Test*. And the host was debonair Food Network chef, *Gourmet* columnist, cookbook author, and all-around know-it-all David Rosengarten.

Brent handed out a multiple-choice quiz that confirmed Rosengarten's involvement – and wiped out any possible connection with *Pressure Cooker*. This brain-spinner was a collision of kindergarten and post-doctoral research levels. What cheese is a specialty of Spain? (Asiago? No, manchego.) Where are white truffles found? (Darn! Italy.) What was the 1920s creation by a chef at Saratoga Springs? (Potato chips; lucky guess!) What type of meat is served as a crown roast? (No pork on the list, so how 'bout… lamb?) Which of the following is cruciferous? (Broccoli, where are you???) What was the name of the *Happy Days* hangout? (Whew.) In what order were popcorn, Pop Tarts, and Pop Rocks introduced? (What you said.)

And so on, for three agonizing pages, in which pop culture ran smack into mega-snootiness. All around me people reeled, vocally, in the impact. "I didn't get half the questions," whined a fresh culinary school graduate. The *Happy Days* question was unfair, complained a man who looked old enough to be retired. The exception to this communal bonding in misery sat to my right. My slender young neighbor confided that she knew that white truffles come from Italy, because she'd studied there when she was at Sarah Lawrence, and she loves food. In fact, she would love to be a restaurant reviewer; she's eaten in all of the best restaurants in Manhattan – her parents give her the money for it – so she should be a reviewer. I stared, speechless, as if at a museum specimen.

She made the first cut. So did I, along with six other people, including the older man. Our next task was playing a game, so Brent could observe how well we followed rules. (Not particularly well, in the case of two of the men.) The game involved passing a videotape around the table until the person who was "it" clapped and said a letter of the alphabet. Whoever had or was taking the tape then tried to name five objects starting with that letter, before the tape made it once around the table. Only one person came up with five words in time, though Miss Sarah Lawrence and I each managed to  spit out four. One of the men (who radiated self-satisfaction) instinctively tossed the tape across the table when he got caught by a clap, while the older guy purposefully delayed a pass to give me a shot at a fifth word.

Our final challenge was talking, which presented me with unexpected (and uncharacteristic) difficulty. Brent asked us to tell a bit about ourselves and share a food-related memory. One person confessed to a life-long aversion to artichokes, which she understood only after learning she'd eaten a box full as a toddler and thrown them all up. One woman bragged about being the only person at college to stock a dorm refrigerator with white wine and brie. The two oldest people took the route of modesty (although the man, who turned out to be a retired butcher, did confess to working in a soup kitchen on holidays). Not the tape-tosser, who indulged in a smug, suspiciously polished yarn of undertaking an investigation after restaurant after restaurant had served him bread that was burnt on the bottom. (The culprit? Sullivan Street Bakery.) Miss Sarah Lawrence credited a love of food from her switching from a college program in England after classmates started talking about going to Italy. She recreated her decision: "Hmmmm...cold weather, bad food...warm weather, good food!"

As for me, well, I blithered. Reducing my complicated, all-pervasive relationship with food to one anecdote eluded me, so I rambled in the hopes that something sparkling would surface. (It did, two days later. Chasing my sister from the dinner table, out the door, and down the block before she realized that the threatening contents of my clenched fist weren't spinach as she feared, but a wadded-up napkin.) People laughed a lot, but I left convinced I'd blown any chance of being called back.

Two phone calls from Brent suggested otherwise. The first was full of perky questions. Do I wear glasses? What's my height? (What is the host, a shrimp? I wondered.) Do I have any food allergies? The second brought definitive word: I had been chosen as the alternate for the last two shows in the series. My reaction relieved Brent. (Other candidates, he said, had actually taken offense at the offer and refused to accept.)

In a novel, that statement would be called foreshadowing.

The day of taping put me in close quarters with six people who showed no signs of a deficit in the self-esteem department (One third-place winner would cap the day by openly deriding his prize.) My job was simply to sit around for five hours in case one of the contestants didn't go on camera. It had happened twice already, Brent told us, but it didn't on my watch. He also related that the producers had tested more than 500 candidates (and asked some 200 to play the tape-passing game), before narrowing the field to 120 finalists, from whom they chose 60 contestants and 11 alternates. Miss Sarah Lawrence was not among them. I asked.

We spent the majority of the afternoon confined in a windowless room that was probably 12 by 13, with a short couch, a love seat, a semi-circle of folding chairs, a mirror, a TV and VCR, and long work tables along two walls. Immediately outside was a small office for the contestant wranglers and, beyond that, a long hallway into which we could venture only with an escort. (The hallway led to the restrooms, the studio, and, most importantly, the "invisible wall" that blocked cubbyhole offices and food preparation areas. Walking through the wall spelled immediate disqualification.)

The main element of décor was food, and mostly junk food at that. Tables in the hallway were strewn with open bags of chips and cookie packages, Hershey's miniatures, bowls of pretzels, and tiny, nearly empty cartons of hummus. The desk in the outer office wasn't much tidier, or healthier. Everywhere you looked lay a cornucopia of preservatives, a lot of which ended up on plates coming into our room.

Brent, himself, munched on baby carrots. "I'm not really into food," he admitted.

He was our cheerful and omnipresent guide through the four main parts of the day. The first chunk was learning the game. It began with two rounds of culinary questions. The two higher scorers would then alternate trying to identify ingredients in a gourmet dish (hence the show's name, *Taste Test*). The survivor had to field 60 seconds' worth of rapid-fire questions in two pre-selected categories. Fourteen right answers would win the grand prize, a trip to some luxurious destination.

To demonstrate the rules in action, Brent showed a video of the first episode. The room exploded with laughter at the foreboding sight of three unsmiling figures clad in all black, nervously shifting from side to side. (So that explained the previous week's phone call countermanding the initial directive to wear black!) Compared to the audition test, the show's questions were on par with elementary school. My companions yelled out answers throughout the video. Nobody got it right when a contestant suggested that menudo is served at New Year's in Mexico City for good luck.

After we watched the first finalist sputter away his chance for the grand prize, Brent rattled off the categories of choices for each of the day's shows and made the contestants commit on the spot. Two that were chosen were whether specific candy contained nuts and whether a food was a good source of Vitamin C. Nobody touched whether certain chips were made from corn or potatoes, or matching fast food items with their restaurants.

Next came a walk-through in the studio. Half of the cavernous space was filled with folding chairs on risers, going up the back wall. The front had a center entrance and runway, one podium on the left, and three contestants' tables on the right. Off the set were two tableaux of artfully arranged goodie baskets, which would later get screen time as prize displays. Brent assigned each contestant a stand and blocked every possible movement, including how losers would leave the set. Everyone stood and walked and mashed on the answer button. I just watched.

Then it was back to confinement, to await a visitation by the host. Smiling, affable, and of a decidedly non-shrimp stature, Rosengarten arrived just before each taping with the head writer and director in tow. As he chatted with each contestant, the trio openly searched (and often pushed) for the angle on what would be a 10-second introduction.

For the first show's contestants, ethnic heritage was enough. An Italian-Jewish marriage had to mean a shared love of Chinese food. (Because of the noodles, the assumption was.) Wouldn't it be funny if the actress with the Italian background riffed on dishes she would prepare if Rosengarten came for dinner? (It wasn't.)

No matter that he'd been brought up by hotelier parents in Europe, the information that he was Swedish irreversibly pigeonholed the man who was already putting up with a misspelled name tag. This upbringing was a surprise to the rest of us, who'd sat around speechless when he'd arrived late, immediately asked whether there was a bar backstage, and, within minutes, pressed a resume onto a competitor when he heard she was in the same industry. Where did this heritage lead Rosengarten? To Swedish meatballs. Mislabeled as "Russ," Rustin had no difficulty improvising – and reprising – a believable tirade against the dish, which he obviously considered an atrocity.

The other round of interviews, just before the second show's taping, was equally revealing and far less ramrodded. It also confirmed my impression of the long-haired, bent-nosed blond in an Italian suit, who looked like Gerard Depardieu's surfer cousin.

"Do you surf?" began Rosengarten.

"Duuuuuuuude," came the reply.

"Solid," Rosengarten answered. He toyed with using the interchange on air, but opted instead for asking about luaus on Long Island. (The surfer digs a pit outside his house and roasts a pig while he and party guests surf.) There was, unfortunately, no inquiry into the financial underpinnings of such a lifestyle.

Publishing two diet cookbooks when she weighed 200 pounds was the hook for a petite and very slender writer with majorly messy upswept hair. (My first reaction to her had been that she needed to get herself in front of a mirror and fix her hair. When we were both in the restroom during a break, she walked out the door without a look – while bemoaning how hard it had been to work a trip to the hairdresser into the morning's schedule. She had paid to look like that.) "Do as I say, not as I eat," became her punchline.

"Some people get 15 minutes; we got nine seconds," quipped Brad, an architect whose guilelessness derailed an attempt to mold his story. "I want to hear more names of Italian foods," interjected the director when Rosengarten quizzed Brad about shopping for produce in Florence. Problem was, Brad didn't know any other names, because he'd bought only foods he knew. He ended up being saddled with a lame comparison of high-rise food and buildings (the gist being that food tastes better), which fell flat on camera.

Actually, most of the patter did. Everyone's sparkle dimmed in the tapings, which I found strangely anti-climactic. I sat on the lip of the first riser while the capacity audience was whipped into a happy and vocal frenzy by a stand-up comedienne. (Rosengarten, handling the final warm-up himself, drew the biggest laugh for giving the audience permission to say anything in the studio but "Bam!", the trademark of Food Network superchef Emeril Lagasse.)

From the moment I learned that London was the first grand prize destination I wanted, finally, to be in the thick of competition myself. German wines? I could nail that. (No one touched the category.) Eventually frustration slid into outright amusement over the persistent, endemic ignorance about food from other parts of the country. Someone actually suggested that the proper addition to a bottle of RC Cola was pork rinds (and looked appalled when she heard peanuts)!

Even better was watching two New Yorkers circle around a mysterious presence in the first tasting round (both of which featured Southwestern dishes, by the way). Was it mint? Basil? Parsley? No, it was cilantro, and neither of them got it.

This round went off course when Russ broke the rules by trying to pass. (The fact that he was dominating the competition after being such a buffoon backstage infuriated the first loser, who sat by me after leaving the set and railed against him.) Taping stopped; a conference broke out; the food was removed and replaced with fresh, hot dishes. The round began again, with the contestants repeating exactly what they had said the first time. When the time came for Russ to correct his error, he didn't even look at the camera but continued eating, slowly, methodically, until the taping stopped and a stagehand reached for the plate.

A flubbed word also shut down the first endgame midway through. Unrattled, the actress recreated her performance flawlessly and went on to win the trip. A technical error scrubbed the second tasting round as well, which like the others, started over from the top.

During the breaks, the stage crew made plans for a wrap party featuring margaritas; one technician loudly expounded on the quality of the food at Henson Productions tapings – and, in my direction, of the superiority of gaffers, such as he, as romantic partners. Brent stopped by to assure me that all the alternates were guaranteed spots as contestants if the network picks up the show for another 22 episodes.

The second taping ended with the cookbook author nabbing the grand prize, a weekend in Santa Fe, and the studio erupted with a general air of elation.

Back in the waiting room, minions from the show cornered us with releases, which had to be signed and photocopied before our prizes would materialize.

"This is all?" sneered the surfer, turning over two huge blocks of Vermont cheese that were nested in an attractive Shaker basket. Even though he'd placed third, he'd pulled off something that had impressed even Rosengarten, correctly identifying three types of water, including Evian and NYC tap, with only one sip each.

Second place winner Brad, sitting on the floor, stacked blocks of cheese into a tall arch as he mused about throwing a dinner party to use up the edible portion of his stash. (He'd also got a coffee table book and a cooking course.)

And my gift? Handed over by a young man who'd moved up a year ago from San Antonio, it was a Southwestern cookbook. I howled.

EPILOGUE

In June 1999 the Food Network quietly debuted a quiz show designed to test the knowledge – and taste buds – of foodie know-it-alls. I've yet to get the call offering me a buzzer of my own. As far as I know, the first 20 episodes are in perpetual rerun, a not-unprecedented phenomenon in the recycling-happy world of cable TV.

After the premiere, I saw some of my contestant companions once again, in a QuickTime video clip of the final episode on the network's website. (The clip's gone now, so you won't be able to see for yourself the winner who would voluntarily turn down accommodations at the five-star Inn of the Anasazi in Santa Fe.)

I don't watch *Taste Test* myself, actually. The reason I turn on the Food Network is *Iron Chef*, a deadly earnest Japanese culinary competition with a flamboyant host and weirdly dubbed commentary fit for an athletic event. Now that's entertainment.

My Table, 2002

> *"Life is too short for self–hatred and celery sticks."*
>
> — Marilyn Wann

MARTHA & ME:
IMPROVISING BROWNIES

I used to see Martha Stewart as a tormentor of womankind — her minutiae-focused approach to modern living prescribing an impossibly manicured standard so unattainable that it would only add to the reasons modern media give women to feel bad about themselves.

Her mature, responsible, and community-bettering handling of her jail sentence turned my opinion into respect. Her *Martha Stewart Living* is one of my few remaining print subscriptions, and the only publication I continue to hoard. The recipes are part of the reason. They exist in the real world, with ingredients that are reasonably easy to acquire (unlike the rarities-to-absurdities that *Gourmet* often invoked), techniques that are within the grasp of mere mortals, and results that both work and taste good. Which leads me to the Double-Chocolate Brownies in the April 2010 issue.

The issue's been with me less than four weeks and I've already made them that many times. They're spectacular, one of the best brownie recipes I've used and definitely the easiest. The double whammy consists of bittersweet chocolate and cocoa powder, and the ease comes from whisking all the eggs and dry ingredients directly into the pan containing the melted chocolate and butter. The result comes out of the oven so wonderfully moist that jostling it (by prematurely lifting the parchment out of the pan or, say, um, cutting away a nibble) causes the perfect crust to crackle with a landscape of canyons.

These brownies require patience, though; the true wonder of their taste does not shine through until they've cooled completely. One recipient pronounced them so good that he wondered whether eating them behind the wheel constituted driving under the influence.

I can't link you to the recipe, but I can walk you through a variation I made when the urge for another batch surfaced late yesterday evening. I went into it knowing I was out of bittersweet chocolate, but did I run out to the store? No. Impulsiveness met laziness and improvisation ensued. Semi-sweet morsels and espresso powder made an acceptable substitute for the bittersweet chocolate. Light and dark Kayro syrup were an experiment, when the sugar ran a half a cup short. The changes required more time in the oven and the dark syrup made for a molasses-y punch when the brownies were warm. Once cooled, these have a harder, crunchy crust, top and bottom, satisfyingly strong chocolaty goodness and an ever-so-slightly sweet aftertaste.

Moon in the 6th, 2010

DOUBLE CHOCOLATE BROWNIES

Preheat oven to 350.

Heat in a double boiler (or a pan/bowl over a pan with water):
    1 stick unsalted butter, cut up
    6 oz semi-sweet morsels
    1 tbs espresso powder

Remove from burner. Whisk in:
    1 cup sugar
    ¼ cup light corn syrup
    ¼ cup dark corn syrup
        (leave out corn syrup if you have 1½ cup sugar on hand)
    3 eggs, one at a time
    ¼ cup unsweetened cocoa powder
    sprinkling of salt (target is ½ tsp)
    ½ cup plus 2 TBS all-purpose flour

Line an 8-inch square baking pan with parchment paper. Pour in batter. Bake 40-45 minutes, until a toothpick comes out close to clean. Let the pan cool, about 15 minutes. Lift the parchment from the pan (here's where the MSL recipe cracks), place it on a wire rack, and let it cool completely.

THE SECRET LIFE OF . . .
BETTY CROCKER?

One of our most enduring culinary icons was an unintended consequence of an advertising promotion for a bag of flour. In 1921 the Minneapolis-based Washburn Crosby Company ran a full-page ad-cum-contest on the back cover of the *Saturday Evening Post*. The contest offered a Gold Medal Flour pincushion as the reward for cutting up a picture puzzle and reassembling the pieces into a quaint street scene. Along with the expected entries – some 30,000 – came hundreds of pleas for baking advice. Having been so dramatically informed of a previously unsuspected consumer need, the company's advertising staff jumped to fulfill it.

And so began Betty Crocker, a figure who grew to be so looming in the American psyche that the lobby of her namesake test kitchens initially kept tissues on hand, so frequently did pilgrims burst into tears at the revelation that she did not exist in the flesh. That one quick decision to birth a helpful, trustworthy kitchen advisor led to developments that still affect kitchens today – including the standardization of baking pan sizes and photograph-laden step-by-step instructions in cookbooks. In the process, she provided jobs for a lot of women (the company's traveling demonstrators, as well as the college graduates who staffed its Home Services Department) and shored up countless more. She dispensed household tips, marital advice, and moral support in a radio show and, later, shorts; when World War II came, she waged a full-tilt morale-boosting campaign championing the patriotic contribution of the homemaker. And as she morphed into a brand for baking preparations, she weaned her followers off her advice and preached the reliability of boxed mixes.

Her evolving existence and impact on both American society and the food industry fill the lively pages of *Finding Betty Crocker: The Secret Life of America's First Lady of Food* by Susan Marks. The book, released by Simon & Schuster, is a brisk, light-handed, and fascinating social history. The gallery of Betty through the ages is especially fun, as are the reproductions.

LLRX.com, 2005

"In general, I think, human beings are happiest at table when they are very young, very much in love or very alone."

— M.F.K. FISHER

TABLE FOR ONE

I enjoy eating alone. No one has a say but the voices in my head, and when they're in charge, anything's possible.

Steamed broccoli for breakfast. Eggs and sausage for dinner, or maybe just a piece of fruit. Cookies during meal prep, and during the meal, and after, too, if they're still appealing. Who knows, I might even make food choices and combinations that match just about anyone's definition of a proper meal, which is actually what happens most of the time. Predictability isn't the goal. Happy-making tastes are, and all the better if they arrive with fun and adventure on the side.

The freedom is what I appreciate most. It's liberating to assemble a meal and eat without concern for another person's needs, expectations, or reactions. If I cook for someone or suggest a restaurant, I go to trouble to come up with something that meets that person's tastes. (I left political cooking behind in my 20s, when a then-frequent dining companion not so wrongly interpreted my reliance on *The Vegetarian Epicure* as foisting an agenda on my guests.) This approach is not so much due to codependency, though a touch may well be involved; it just strikes me as considerate and good manners. If I'm the only one who's going to eat, on the other hand, my tastes are all that matter. I'll try experiments and make substitutions to which I would never subject anyone else. (*What, no olive oil? What if I seared that pork chop in... pinot noir vinegar?*)

Fortunately, I'm not finicky.

Fending for myself is not only liberating; it's relaxing. I don't have to impress anyone, be an expert, or contend with someone's judgments, assumptions, or insecurities. I get to eat for myself and as myself, and not as a food writer, a persona that has a way of popping up after hours whether I invite her or not. The label stirs complex emotions in some people, often a jumble of envy, intimidation, and something that looks like awe. Once a filter like that locks in, any shared meal, even any restaurant suggestion — especially any restaurant suggestion — can lead to uncomfortable complications (home cooks asking "Are you going to review this meal?" and laughing nervously, very nervously) and backsplash on your professional competence and reputation. When I'm alone, the dynamics are simpler. They're just me and food and whatever is going on in my head.

It's also relaxing not to be bound by anyone else's timetable. I eat when I want, not when any clock says it's time, except for maybe the one in my stomach. (Interestingly, I have discovered that the most rigid by-the-clock eater in my acquaintance drops the practice when her spouse leaves town, a revelation that speaks volumes about the games our minds can play on ourselves when other people are at the table.) I don't normally think about food until I'm ready to deal with it. I usually decide on the spur of the moment what I'm going to eat, instead of haggling over a menu and timetable hours in advance, as other people have pressured me to do. I'm often happy to decide based on what's in the pantry and fridge, but I'll go out to the store or to a restaurant if a particular craving is strong enough. Some people can't live with this lack of certainty and planning. Experience has made me confident that even if I have no idea in the morning what my supper will be, there is always something to eat come evening.

Back to cravings: that subject feeds directly into one of the prime perks of eating alone, indulging in guilty pleasures. Everyone has foods and behaviors they prefer to keep on the downlow, and it's easy to succumb to their charms when eating unsupervised. That's part of the allure, actually, giving in for no better reason than no one is going to shame or stop you. I can make a meal of chips and homemade guacamole or allot a disproportionate share of the day's calories to chocolate without anyone raising an eyebrow or ever knowing. I can douse scrambled eggs with ketchup without prompting anyone to leave the table (there's precedent) or eat from a container at the kitchen counter without hearing *Put it on a plate; it'll taste better*. I can even deliberately, repeatedly ingest items that friends would swear I never touch, foods that *Nutrition Action* tells me to shun, foods like...tater tots. Eaten daily, until the bag runs out. For breakfast, even.

Sometimes — most of the time, thank goodness — the motive has nothing to do with placating a demanding inner toddler. Sometimes the drive is completely utilitarian. *I am hungry. How can I fix that?* When the point of eating is stripped to that basic impulse, the actual substance of the meal is less important than the means to it, preferably as quickly as possible. To me,

leftovers are an ideal solution. Take them out of the container, heat them if necessary, and presto! It's time to eat. So what if that means eating the same thing twice within a day or two? If I liked something enough to save it, I can generally raise my boredom threshold to accommodate a repeat experience (often as early as the next morning,

a proclivity I can directly trace to restaurant reviewing). Besides, if abating hunger is really the goal, leftovers offer a compelling economy of time and effort, not to mention money.

Even when hunger pangs are not on red alert, I rarely go to as much trouble for myself as I will for others. Certain dishes I'll make from a recipe, but more often than not I improvise. A couple of tortillas, beans, and grated cheese suffice at times; at others, the answer is a salad with a jumble of differently textured vegetables and a piece of salmon on top.

I eat better and with greater variety (I am peculiarly prone to ruts; see tater tots confession above) when I buy chicken, meat, and fish in bulk and freeze them in single-serve parcels. I haven't gone as far as friends who prepare elaborate entrees on the weekend and portion them into meal-sized Ziplock bags, but I have come up with a technique for whipping up a cooked-from-scratch meal on short notice. I saute onions while something from the freezer is defrosting in the microwave. Based on what I've chosen, I throw celery and garlic into the skillet, or maybe mushrooms, or sliced apples if it's pork. Then I add the thawed protein and heat it till cooked, sometimes poaching it in juice or dark beer, or sharpening the savoriness with a marinade or balsamic vinegar. In the meantime, I might steam vegetables (broccoli or cauliflower are common), assemble a salad, perhaps nuke a small potato or yam.

Sometimes I leave the freezer shut and use the sauteed onions instead as the base for an elaborate expansion of scrambled eggs, filled out with celery, thinly sliced zucchini, carrot shavings, and some sort of greens. Unpretentious, to be sure (although some variations have turned out stunningly), but the technique usually shoe-horns easily into my schedule and reliably delivers an honest, balanced, home-cooked meal. When I go to this effort for only myself, all the voices in my head are happy – all the more so if I eat at the table like a civilized person, rather than in front of the TV or (shhh, guilty secret coming) beside the laptop.

Eating solo in public is a different story. The fact that you're sitting alone becomes inescapably obvious when other people are around. It probably doesn't matter to anyone who might notice, assuming anyone even would. It's a common enough phenomenon for both genders now, unlike three decades ago, when I read an op-ed piece that constructed a feminist manifesto out of the writer's daring to go to restaurants by herself. (It was Dallas, after all, where she'd already earned street cred as an undergraduate for defying convention by openly living with a professor.) Most people I know are perfectly comfortable with grabbing a bite on their own, without concern for what the staff or other customers might think.

Solitariness has yet to be an issue for me in the sorts of casual places I go by myself – diners, delis, coffee shops, down-home cafes, burger and barbecue joints, low-key restaurants that don't require reservations. Even so, my tendency is to get in and out without dawdling (and leave a generous tip), unless some factor is compelling enough to warrant hanging around. Particularly good people-watching will keep me in my seat; ordering dessert has proven to be an effective cover for prolonging eavesdropping when nearby conversations have headed into the makings of a cable TV script. Writing can also extend my stay.

That time-honored coffeehouse tradition also works in cafes, where it's helped me stretch my enjoyment of a pizza, and even a single serving of whipped cream-topped pumpkin bread once, into well over an hour.

Lingering over a

meal for its own sake comes more naturally to me on the road. It's easier there to turn off the auto-pilot that takes us through so much of life, sharpen my perceptions, and sink deeply into each moment. If hunger hits when I'm out and about on my home turf, I'll drop into the closest acceptable place; if it happens when I'm traveling, I walk around a neighborhood, read menus, peer into dining rooms, and consciously tell myself I can eat anywhere I please. (Yes, this approach deserves a place in everyday living.) Taking a meal offers more than physical nourishment when the setting is a different city, a different part of the country, or a different country altogether. Every aspect of the experience has food for the senses: the singular décor, the dress and appearance of the staff and customers, the sound of the voices, the unique textures and tastes of the butter, the bread, and each new dish that arrives. The knowledge that I may not repeat the experience easily, or ever, heightens my awareness of its value and disinclines me to rush it to an end. I would not take in so many details if my attention were split between them and conversation with a companion. I don't feel lonely at all; I feel lucky to be alone.

That gusto doesn't carry over into dining alone in a fine restaurant. That experience has a similarly to-be-cherished nature, but strangely, it does not hold the same appeal. Or any, actually. I have never had dinner alone in a restaurant refined enough to require reservations, much less one that has been awarded a star. Circumstances haven't required it (somehow, it's never been a problem finding a companion for an elegant meal, especially when a publication was picking up the tab), and I have felt no urge to try it out on my own. Thrift is one reason, but no doubt there are others.

No matter where it takes place, the experience of eating alone leads directly to the question of how comfortable you are with your own company, which is to say, with yourself. The prospect makes some people uneasy. When no one's around to provide a buffer, they'll enlist other distractions to ward off awareness or, perish forfend, examination of the self. Watching TV or reading

magazines, newspapers, the backs of cereal boxes – it's all an equivalent of white noise, blocking out whatever is on the inside.

When people share food, especially if one of them was the cook, the subtext usually runs something like this: *Let me prove my love to you with this delicious meal, and you can prove your love in return by eating. A lot. Second or third helpings, please.* Funny how the exchange-of-love aspect of eating disappears when only one person is at the table. Have you ever sensed this kind of motivation in meals you've had by yourself? I certainly haven't. My growing penchant for cooking full meals is a start, but I still accord other people a lot more consideration in the kitchen than I give myself.

The exchange is possible, though. I've heard of one person who mastered it. He was a coworker of a friend of mine in a design studio a few decades back. Each day at lunch the coworker would pull out a tablecloth, napkin, plate, flatware, candlestick, and a single wine glass, the only one he owned. After arranging the table, he would set out and calmly eat a full meal he'd prepared the night before. (Add to the novelty of this scene the fact that the coworker was a black man in a largely Caucasian company.)

One day my friend asked why he went to all this trouble. The answer?

Because I deserve it.

The voices in my head are still chewing on that one.

SKILLET SUPPER

The basic formula is:

Look in the freezer.

Select protein (chicken/pork chop/fish/ground meat/veggie burger).

Saute onions in olive oil while thawing protein in microwave.

Add protein, salt, pepper, and seasoning.

Heat till done.

VARIATIONS

Add minced garlic, sliced mushrooms, tomatoes or fruit (sliced apples on pork, orange sections on fish)

Use flavored oil (I like basil or Asian chili oil from Boyajian)

Douse the protein with a balsamic or flavored vinegar. (This obviously will not work with ground meat or veggie burgers.)

Poach protein in orange, lime or tomato juice, a microbrew or wine. (Ditto.)

Sprinkle your protein with a marinade or finishing sauce; flip to coat both sides.

SCRAMBLED EGG VARIATION

Skip freezer step and remove two eggs from the fridge.

As the onions soften, add your choice of produce: chopped celery, minced garlic, diced tomatoes, sliced mushrooms, slivered carrots, thinly sliced zucchini, broccoli florets.

Loosely beat the eggs, lower the heat, then pour the eggs into the skillet. Scramble gently.

Add snippets of basil, thyme, chives; a handful of spinach or baby greens.

Scramble some more. Season to taste.

My Table, 2009

*"Food is our
common ground,
a universal
experience."*
—James Beard

EATING OUT IS FUN!

While running errands during the noon lunch hour last fall, I made a split-second decision to get lunch at a Russian deli I hadn't visited for a couple of years. Yakov's Deli was just far enough outside my normal peregrinations that it rarely came to mind, but when it did, it always delivered a good meal, cheap, and often much more.

The owners are Soviet emigrés — the husband the kitchen-bound executive chef, as numerous framed certificates and articles attest, the wife everything else, from cashier to counter help to front woman extraordinaire. She astonished me once by correctly reciting to a newcomer I'd brought in exactly what I had ordered on my previous visit one-and-a-half years earlier; another time, she generously agreed to translate a letter a friend had received from a Russian paramour. She followed through when a cursory read-through should have made it clear that the sender was as female as my friend sitting with us. As our translator rattled off a string of memories and declarations of future desires, I sensed an omission. "Isn't that 'I want to kiss you'?" I asked, pointing to a verb. "More than kissing!" she announced, handing back the letter. We all laughed ourselves into red-faced hysterics.

This day I had no mission other than lunch. True to form, the proprietress greeted me like a long-lost friend. As I settled on my order, I realized out of nowhere that the place had just been named to the Houston Press' Best of

Houston Hall of Fame. I asked if she knew. She didn't.

"You got best borscht," I explained. Borscht isn't exactly free-flowing in Houston, but she didn't care. She put her hand on her chest, shut her eyes, and swallowed. "He deserves it," she gushed, patting herself proudly and comfortingly. She ran around the counter, threw her arms around what she could reach of me (I'm close to a foot taller), and put her head on my chest. "Thank you," she said, reverently, looking up with palpable emotion, not to mention misplaced gratitude. Remembering that a spare copy of the issue was in my front seat, I extracted myself to fetch the paper. She opened it hungrily; seeing the words of honor, she summoned her husband from the kitchen.

Not only had I never seen him out front, I'd never heard him talk. The excitement of this news stirred him to oratory. Of course he should be best borscht! He is best of everything in all Houston! Last year Joel's Deli got best sandwich – for *chicken salad?* (I winced; I'd written the current best sandwich award for a chicken and artichoke concoction.) That's not best sandwich! *He* has best sandwich![3]

As he wove his passionate tapestry, his wife slipped in the invitation to select anything I wanted in the case as a dessert, on them. Before I could, he handed over an enormous chocolate bar and floridly bestowed sweetness in

return for the sweetness I'd brought them. Finally, they sent me to my seat in a cloud of thank-yous.

Yakov was too agitated to return to the anonymity of his kitchen. He gave a guided tour of a wall of framed reviews, awards, and photographs to the president of his corporate, soon-to-be-ex landlord (the strip center was changing ownership), who'd been finishing lunch during the earlier outburst.

---

[3] The Moscow, for anyone close enough to try one; it's like a club sandwich on a huge French roll with really creamy dressing and, yes, it is a veritable taste treat.

He materialized at my table while I was eating and asked me to explain the Hall of Fame's subtitle: "100 Things You Can Count On Year After Year." Once he understood, he embraced it with a vengeance and launched into a tirade about placing more importance on honor and integrity than making money. ("I have conscious!" he stressed repeatedly.)

And when, finally, a new customer walked in, he loudly recommended the day's special, which was, of course, borscht. "Best borscht in Houston!" he announced, whapping the back of his hand onto the Hall of Fame page as proof.

"I love you!" his wife yelled, waving as I picked up my stuff to leave. I felt like I was walking out of a Frank Capra movie – which, in a sense, I was.

The Houston Press Bests paid off again later in the week. A couple of pals and I decided to do something with Friday evening other than knock back Coronas and Negra Modelos. The idea was trying a west-side warehouse district restaurant that was supposed to have decent Southern cooking, according to the daily paper. I'd already checked out the place for breakfast, which uniformly smacked of Pam, but the spirit of camaraderie prevailed and opened my mind about the possibility of dinner. Besides, there was supposed to be live music.

Our planned expedition quickly proved to be beside the point. The place was strangely deserted; most of the staff was hanging out at the bar and the only other customers (not to mention white folk), were two senior citizens who'd have looked more at home at a bait camp. They stared at the floor and brought their chewing to an end when the band finally finished setting up and started playing. The fried chicken and chicken-fried steak were passable, and laudably Pam-free. The blues band was better, if only for the incongruity of a physically and musically wimpy white guy fronting three more than respectable black musicians.

Still, both food and entertainment left us wanting. After a moment's churning, my internal amusement generator[4] spit out the solution: Carriage Creamery, an ice cream shop in a converted gas station a few miles down the street. The very exterior exuded happiness. A warm glow spilled out of the chunky white building. Strings of little white lights glittered around columns at the front. As we stepped from the car, Eastern European accordion music wafted on the wind. It accompanied us to the doorway, where an accordion and recorder were noodling away.

Inside, the options were overwhelming, easily two dozen vats of ice cream and ices in extraordinary concoctions laden with chocolate and mocha and tropical fruits. We chose our indulgences in twos and threes and went slack-jawed as the clerk rang up each serving of multiple scoops for the price of one small. "We were voted Best Ice Cream," she beamed, pointing to a laminated *Houston Press* clipping lying by the cash register. "So I'm celebrating!" As she rang mine up, I caught sight of a coconut cake nearly a foot tall. Its perfect shape radiated, "Come to me;" my purchase cautioned, "Are you out of your mind?" If there's room, I thought, wistfully.

In the carport turned front porch, we sat amid twinkling lights, airborne windsocks, and clusters of happy, smiling people. The music turned to Parisian, Piaf standards mostly, and we swayed along, marveling at the tastiness of our choices, marveling still more at the server's generosity and giving a moment of silence each time a piece of massive coconut cake entered our vision. It was a perfect night.

Ladies' Fetish & Taboo Society
Compendium of Urban Anthropology, 1998

---

[4] References available on request; access available on my whim and what you're offering. Let's tawk.

"Food is not about impressing people. It's about making them feel comfortable."

— INA GARTEN

EVER-WIDENING
CONCENTRIC CIRCLES OF YUM

This concept grew out of a phone call with a geographically distant friend who enjoys talking about preparing food. When she heard that arroz con pollo was on the menu for my household that day, she gasped that the dish was one of her husband's favorites and asked if we'd send the recipe. Sure; it's just the basic recipe from the Goya[5] website, the cook pointed out after I hung up. Maybe not just that, I thought.

And so, I made sure what we sent was more. The cook humored my request to type up the recipe as he actually makes it. Simply dropping that into the mail still didn't seem like enough. I looked over the ingredients and realized that a couple of the seasonings were not likely to be easy for my friend to come by in her normal shopping flight path. I picked up a large container of each, packed them in a box with the recipe on top and shipped them off.

A few days later, my friend happily reported that her husband was at that moment making several meals' worth of arroz con pollo. She, on the other hand, was already brainstorming additional uses for the adobo seasoning blend and also planning to introduce another cook to it. What started as a gift

[5] When I wrote this, the brand had no political charge whatsoever.

from one kitchen to another looked to be spreading to more destinations than originally foreseen. Yum, we agreed. Ever-widening concentric circles of yum, I realized, and thus this second campaign was born.

At least once in the coming year, I hope you'll join me in sharing a dish that you especially enjoy – not a high-maintenance item from a demanding cookbook, but real-life food that you have actually prepared more than a time or two. The point is not making and handing over a finished product, but helping someone else make it for him- or herself.

Don't wait for a special occasion; in fact, doing this when there's nothing on the calendar will make the gesture stand out all the more. Write up the recipe, with your own personal tips and experiences, and tuck it into a box with a couple of key or non-staple ingredients. Ship the package off to a friend or relation, and think of the home-cooked goodness spreading from your kitchen to another and points beyond.

LLRX.com, 2005

REGIONAL FAVORITES:
MINERS' FARE IN NORTHERN NJ

Rocky's Pasties has been on my mind for the past few days. It's a one-of-a-kind takeout counter specializing in the unpretentious meal-in-a-pocket called a Cornish pasty, a single-serving, dough-encased pie along the lines of an empanada (only bigger) or a calzone (only smaller, and without cheese or sauce). The item is definitely low-to-invisible in the ranks of this country's melting pot cuisines and below the mainstream radar even here in Rocky's home base of north central New Jersey. I learned about the store from an ad-cum-coupon on a diner place mat, of all things. My first visit years ago delivered magic with staying power, from the anachronistically simple signs, to the gnomish counterman who slowly emerged, as if from another place and time, to take and fulfill my order, to the hearty, hardy, and savory treats I unwrapped at home.

The experience wasn't an anomaly. Every return visit has had a gentleness, ease, and open-heartedness that are refreshing to the point of bordering on otherworldly. (When I once mentioned that I was taking a large frozen order out of town, the counterman expressed genuine interest in knowing the destination.) And, of course, it doesn't hurt that the pasties are tasty, too.

So when the weekend brought gloomy skies and an unseasonable return to cool temperatures, I took them as a call for a comfort food pick-me-up and headed to Rocky's. It's in the small town of Wharton, once a mining center (true of so many northern New Jersey towns) that now enjoys a quiet bordering on dreariness. On a residential stretch one block off the main street, Rocky's is in the middle of an unassuming row of townhouses, of the utilitarian and archaic worker residence variety and not remotely resembling the townhouses of the last few decades. Rocky's existence is an outgrowth of the town's mining past. The miner population was heavy on immigrants from the British Isles for whom, word is, a pasty provided a hand-holdable meal that could be carried into the mines. This family-owned business started producing pasties for the community four generations ago.

Rocky's also sells homemade strudels and banana walnut bread, hand-labeled and, by appearances, hand-wrapped as well. These haven't wowed me but have a loyal fanbase of their own; when a friend moved from the town, one particular strudel variety topped her list of things she would miss. The mainstay pasties come in three varieties: beef, sausage or chicken, each filled with neatly cut blocks of potato. My latest sausage purchase had a bit less meat than I remember, but the size is still big (about 4" by 2"-plus), the ingredients remain fresh and the seasonings are lively. The crust is neither thick and rubbery nor thin and flat, but somehow just right. I'll be restocking the freezer again soon.

Moon in the 6th, 2010

"A project is like love; it has clear intentions at the beginning, but it can get complicated."

— GERRY GEEK

ENTERTAINING BY PROJECT MANAGEMENT

The first time I heard my friend Rex Gillit talk about "QA-ing" a dinner party he'd hosted, I feared he'd gone over to the dark side. Dropping an acronym into casual social conversation? As a verb? With no referent, definition, or, even more troubling, hint of amusement?

My concern only grew as he detailed his post-party analysis of his guests' consumption and how the data would affect his next soirée. The explication provided clues, at least. If he was analyzing what people ate, "QA" must mean: Quality Assurance. And that must mean...my friend was applying project management techniques to *entertaining at home*. The realization was chilling: I was sure graduate business school was endangering his soul.

Before this conversation, I would have characterized both of our attitudes toward entertaining as unpretentious. Mine is, admittedly, the more relaxed; I'm from the school of making way too much of everything and have been known to encourage folks to pull up a piece of floor when guests outnumber the conventional seating. Rex's approach has been a bit more proper, but nonetheless down-to-earth, delivering good, sturdy nutritious victuals (and enough chairs), planned with palpable respect for the basic food groups and executed with competence and more attention to the dictates of recipes than I generally give. Neither of us had shown the faintest glimmer of harboring an inner Sue Anne Nivens, poised to portion food out rigidly per guest like some Veal Prince Orloff (the notoriously insufficient entree at perhaps the most disastrous of the dinner parties on The Mary Tyler Moore Show). Until now. I was worried.

I was forgetting a rule for living that Rex and I had developed years ago. It happened when he told me about watching the single most fastidious person in our combined acquaintance empty an ice tray and put it back in the freezer without refilling. Reality warped at the incongruity – *a fussbudget letting something go?* – until the perp explained that he refilled all of his trays at once at a specific time every Saturday afternoon. The universe relaxed into its familiar contours and left us with a guiding principle: When surface appearances make no sense, dig deeper.

So what would drive an experienced cook, generous-hearted host, and expert conversationalist to bring corporate-speak and a spreadsheet – yes, a spreadsheet – into his dining room and kitchen? Not graduate business school, no; it was basic psychology. Put a person under stress, and he will reach for familiar behaviors as a coping mechanism. Rex is compensating for previously unconfessed insecurities about inviting people into his home. And what floors me as much as this realization, as much as the acronym-turned-verb and the revelation of the spreadsheet, is that when I've related this saga to outsiders, the common reaction – once we move past the "huh?" part – has been what you would expect from a migraine sufferer learning that the world's strongest pain reliever has gone over-the-counter. Rex is far from alone in his plight, it turns out, and he's fashioned a cure that appeals strongly to the socially anxious.

What got this rolling was the cause of many a life change and adjustment: buying a house – in this case, one with a layout that's conducive to entertaining en masse. Emboldened by home ownership, Rex and his partner David Opheim invited a dozen people to come over for a celebratory buffet spread.

Then reality hit.

They'd invited people over; lots of them. Rex wanted to provide them with a buffet spread and bar. He could vaguely picture the experience in his mind based on what he'd seen others do, but he didn't know how he was going to make it happen. What he did know was something that would ease the process.

Some people write to-do lists and check off items as they are done. Rex made a spreadsheet.

He plotted out purchases and tracked where they bought each item, how much they bought, and the price they paid. Then he designed the layout of the food and beverage spreads and drew up a schedule of critical tasks. After the guests left, he surveyed what was left on the platters and made corresponding entries onto the spreadsheet. When it was over, his actions looked very much like a procedure he's learned over 20 years as a business analyst-turned-programmer and nonprofit board member: project management.

He swears it wasn't intentional. I'll let him take over from here.

Rex explains: I never thought of this as project management. In retrospect I noticed that a lot of things I did were things that you would do in mapping a moderately complicated project. I'm using skills that I've used successfully for other things in an area where I'm really intimidated. I just didn't want to flop miserably, and the biggest way I could flop was not having something critical, like the forks. This is completely realistic when you're trying to put out this big array of stuff for 12 people. All I was trying to do was make sure I didn't overlook something, and that I had a way to look at what I was projecting and think about it, tweak it, increase things and decrease things and basically come to feel comfortable with it.

Whoa, whoa, whoa – a spreadsheet?

The point of setting something like this up in a spreadsheet is twofold: First, you set it up with key information so that you can sort it differently. You can sort it by the category so that you can figure out all the things that you have and don't have in the paper and cutlery category.

The second reason to put it in a spreadsheet is because that way you can do math on it. For example, you can estimate your costs based on the fact that you'll need 60% less sliced meat the next time as you did this time and roughly project what your cost is going to be. The downside is it doesn't account for things like inflation or mad cow or anything else that can change the price of anything that you do, but it gives you a sense of where your money is going or is expected to go.

Describe this spreadsheet, please.

I set up a column on the left-hand edge that was "Category." That was to group things into functionally similar combinations: food; hard beverages; soft beverages; cutlery and paper and ice and condiments. [The current category labels have been reduced to Food, Bar, Tableware, and Miscellaneous.] The other columns are name of the item, quantity, units the quantity is measured in, quantity meaning quantity purchased, units it's measured in, quantity consumed, for which you could substitute percent consumed if you wanted to, and notes. You should always have a notes column, because that's where you want to point out things like on a mixed deli tray if the roast beef is the only thing that people didn't eat.

For those of you feeling intimidated or overwhelmed or, admit it, judgmental, the "quantity consumed" column contains such precise units of measurement as "a little" and "nibbles."

Let me back up and say one more reason that I did the spreadsheet. This was subconscious, but I think this came directly from project management. In managing projects there are a number of phases involved: a planning phase; a specification phase where you actually write out what the functional use of whatever it is you're doing is going to be; maybe a designing phase where you craft the way that the actual solution is going to work; a programming phase and a unit testing phase and a system testing phase — those are all various levels of integrating the product or service or whatever into the workflow and confirming that everything indeed works and that it doesn't break something else along the way. And what happens after that are the implementation phase and some kind of quality assurance. That's where the greatest variety is in methodology. What you basically want to do is find out what lessons you learned from the project. What went particularly well; what went wrong. What worked; what didn't work. What could you have done differently.

The quality of the way things actually work, or the amount of effort that goes into making them work, depends enormously on the planning and specification phases, because that's where you define what your problem is. And you can't solve a problem until you can state a problem.

Not having had a lot of recent experience with having guests and entertainment and food I knew that I was facing a problem that I couldn't define. That's why I started using the spreadsheet. So that's a question to ask yourself if you're planning an event: "Can I describe clearly what I'm trying to do and what all of the pieces are that are necessary for me to do that?" If you can't, then you should manage it like a project. And start by defining it:

Define what your problem is and your specifications, which are what are all the functional things that should happen. What are the end results, what are the outcomes? People have a good time. People have plenty to eat. People can move around easily. There are places for them to all talk and to rearrange into different groups easily. There's not a traffic obstruction around the food. Stop and think about mechanically how you want the experience to feel for your guests.

At what point in this process do you think about what you're going to serve?

That would probably be in the very beginning, after the definition of it, because the definition is more or less how it has to work. Are Jewish people coming? Are there people who have dietary problems caused by health? Are they teetotalers or are they drinkers? That's part of the specifications: understanding who your guests are and what the needs for each would be.

The spreadsheet was just one tool for managing this. In project management you manage your resources or inputs to the project, which usually include labor and time and money, and if there's a lot of physical stuff to be handled, then it involves managing objects as well.

Did you chart out a timeline of tasks?

I did in preparing the laying out of the food and beverage, because I had a sequence of unrelated events that all had to flow along their appropriate schedule. As an example, I had a large glass bowl that I was going to put out with the ice in it for cocktails. So that it would work well and last longer through the evening without turning into a giant block of fused ice cubes, I wanted to put the bowl into the freezer and get it as cold as I possibly could before I put ice in it. To do that it had to go into the freezer a half an hour to an hour beforehand, and that would be during the time that I was preparing the crudités and starting to line other things up to put them out. So on my spreadsheet I had a separate page that had a task list in order. And it included things like putting the bowl in the freezer and then filling it with ice and putting it back in the freezer at that point and then setting it out so that I wouldn't forget to put the ice out or to do something to have the ice ready to put out.

How did you integrate David into this? Did the established dynamic of your acting as project manager (in the technology company the couple owns jointly) feed into this?

That was an easy part. I printed two copies of the task list out and assigned responsibilities for general parts of it. For example, one of us would take care of getting the large food things put out, like the meat tray and the crudités, and one of us would take care of assembling all the condiments and nibbles and crackers and olives, so that they could be put out. Once they got assembled, they got set onto a staging area and the one of us who was doing the actual final placement would go out and put the stuff out.

For this to work there does need to be a lead person, right?

There does. That became more important during the evening because we had some guests who miscalculated how long it would take to come to our house and called us on the way to let us know that they were going to be here about 25 minutes early. Our response was, that just means you have to help set up. And they said, no problem. So, when they got here, I was able to hand off things on the list to them and that freed up David to go and grab a couple of additional things that we thought might be useful.

So: don't hesitate to take advantage of your guests and press them into service for the task list.

Absolutely not, because to tell you the truth, that helped get this party going. I had a similar experience at the third event that we had here when I also had some people help me set things out and that got people talking and it got rid of the nervousness that is usually in the room at the first.

No matter how much preparation and planning and organization and thought and methodology you put into it, there will be something unexpected that you'll have to deal with. That's true of every project. In this case, it was the fact that one pair of guests ended up having their children who had a two-year-old baby plan a visit to town and wanted to know if it was okay to bring the whole entourage. As it happened they were the ones who arrived 25 minutes early so that gave me a perfect opportunity to figure out how the two-year-old would fit into things. We were able to do a quick round with the mother, to not child-safe the house but at least obviate the most obvious potential problems, like glass things on lower shelves.

What about QA-ing the party?

I went back to the spreadsheet and made note of the quantities of everything that was consumed and what I didn't actually put out and what kind of deli tray, for example. It had slices of turkey, ham, and beef and slices of three kinds of cheese, and virtually all the cheese was gone and about half of the ham and half the turkey were gone and the beef had been virtually untouched. That was useful information. And we did the same thing for cups and plates and dinner and cocktail napkins and fruit and crudités. Crudités mostly just sat there and turned into soup the next week.

The risky part is the beverages. I have a friend, David Weber, who's a programmer/project manager also, who assures me that what happens in terms of beverages does not have any bearing on what will happen the next time. For example, if you stock up on one particular thing because that's what they enjoyed last time, let's say it was gin and tonic, chances are just as good that everyone will drink beer, or everyone will drink red wine, the next time. What I did was record how much of each kind of liquor and how much wine and how much beer and how much of each of the soft drinks we went through so as to try to limit the expense of the next time we had that many people over.

This is essentially a good way for the novice or insecure.

Yes, I think a lot of people would have a larger buffet-style get-together but it scares them. They're terrified that it won't go right, that it will be disastrous, that it will have too little or too much of something and taking an approach like this people can do things that they otherwise might not feel comfortable doing and have a great time doing this.

The whole point of it is — don't shortchange the planning, and don't lose out on the terrific insights you can get after it's over. And if you do it in writing, you can use that to make the next event go better and easier for yourself.

Rex continues to entertain using the spreadsheet and related PM techniques. He reports that one later party was more interesting than the inaugural buffet spread thanks to an Argentina theme, which was reflected in the choice of beverages, table linens, and party favors. He is, however, unable to answer the question, "How much did we oversupply the project?" because he failed to follow through on the "lessons learned" phase and record the amount of supplies consumed. "Fortunately," he notes, "In the case of beverages, there is never a shortage of alternative uses for excess supplies in our organization."

My Table, 2008

"If you accept a dinner invitation, you have a moral obligation to be amusing."

— THE DUCHESS OF WINDSOR

FOOL MOON

During a recent[6] lunar eclipse[7] an omni-directional Scud lust missile detonated at a dinner party and targeted, in sequence, a married man (who was accompanied by his wife), a gay man, and a straight woman, at an unwavering success rate of exactly zero. The final target, who had the misfortune of also being the hostess, doomed to watch her soiree push the concept of an "intimate party" into uncharted territory, ended up giving the exploding guest a ride home, which entailed 30 minutes of coping with a clutch going bad and a passenger grabbing the driver's thigh and exclaiming, "Woman!"

The next morning, the hostess' post office box received an unsolicited

publication entitled "Sweet Tart – the 'zine for and about gratuitously naked ♀♀." Within a day or two, the weary hostess' clutch went out and the car became

[6] "Recent" as in "during this incarnation;" we're hoping we've sat on this goodie long enough to get away with telling it.

[7] Non-astrological grounds advanced in explanation of this occurrence include the solo consumption of a bottle of wine and several martinis, and having gone six weeks without "getting any."

undrivable. A mechanic explained that the slave cylinder had developed a hole and all its lubricant had leaked out, which caused the master cylinder to malfunction. Tell us about it.

Ladies' Fetish & Taboo Society
Compendium of Urban Anthropology, 1994

"*I learned a long time ago that reality was much weirder than anyone's imagination.*"

— HUNTER S. THOMPSON

SLIP SLIDIN' AWAY

Scene: A Chinese-Vietnamese restaurant west of Houston, outside the Beltway. My friend John and I are on a lunch expedition. I have been regaling him with tales of parallel universes masquerading as our own. It all began the day before, when I woke up with a slow swirling in only one ear. After the friend I'd been expecting never showed up, I went on to a movie as planned and inside the theater she leapt across the aisle at me exclaiming that she'd knocked on my front door for 10 minutes. In a late-night phone chat, another friend divulged his own weird equilibrium problems that morning, not to mention someone knocking on his window, with a coin, for 15 minutes that afternoon without him hearing it. John absorbed all this in his usually complacent way.

Partway through the meal, I felt everything lurch sideways. "The world just moved to the right," I said carefully.

"No, it didn't," he responded, and

pointed to my right. "It moved that way."

"You felt it?"

"Uh-huh."

At which point the Muzak broke into a tango.[8] And after that, an instrumental of "Tea For Two," underscored with chants of "tscha, tscha, tscha."[9] Next, "The Blue Danube." Then, an instrumental "Smoke Gets In Your Eyes." Then something too close to "Lady of Spain" for comfort. And so, having slid into the parallel universe in which tangos are played in Asian restaurants, we walked out.

Ladies' Fetish & Taboo Society
Compendium of Urban Anthropology, 1995

---

[8] The one to which Gomez and Morticia Addams dance in *Addams Family Values*.

[9] "It's an Oriental dance tape!" John hooted.

YUMMY, YUMMY, YUMMY, I'VE GOT LOVE IN MY TUMMY

D angling from the ceiling at the Hollywood Food Store are handwritten signs announcing: "I'm from England! Pick me up! I'm from Holland! Eat me! I'm from America! Blow me! I'm from Indonesia! Swallow me! I'm from Australia! Pay me!"

Below these eye-catching exhortations? An entire convenience store aisle of expensive imported chocolates and candies. No, this is not San Francisco. This isn't even California. It's the corner of Hyde Park and Montrose Boulevards, Houston, Texas – across the street from a leather showroom, around the corner from the gay bar district.

Ladies' Fetish & Taboo Society
Compendium of Urban Anthropology, 1994

IT WAS BOUND TO HAPPEN, AND NOW IT HAS

I was hit on in a gay bar. By a man.

Not by a dancer; that's already happened (and not so unusual, by the way). By a customer. And not in a glitzy bar throbbing with a disco beat and bodies on the make. Not even in a bar with a hard liquor license. In a pool hall.

What I was doing there was a favor: performing in a benefit for the Pet Patrol, an organization that cares for the multi-legged loved ones of PWAs. I shared an unventilated dressing room with women donning tuxedos and men filling their bras with stocking-covered bags of birdseed, closures carefully positioned to suggest perky nipples. My condition was singular: my cleavage was unassisted and real; I'd done my own makeup; my hair was my own. In this environment of artificiality, such naturalness was downright perverse.

And only got more so. Before the show, my accompanist Rex (who does always seem to be present at moments worthy of reporting) and I took refuge at one of the few tables with a direct sightline to the stage. It also had an unobstructed view of the door, through which wafted a disturbing number of faces familiar to us. Word of the event had spread through the Gay Men's Chorus of Houston, and several of the usual suspects had stopped in to donate pet food and lend moral support. Dave Weber, relieved by this bar's deficiencies from his usual obligation to lay gin and tonic before me, took the seat next to mine. Instead of welcoming him, Rex and I groused about our friends having gone to the trouble to ferret out this bar; we'd assumed that its obscurity would grant us the luxury of performing under seedy circumstances for people who'd never see us again.

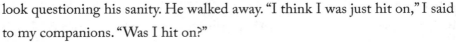

"This is not what I expected!" I exclaimed.

A response came from a man walking by our table. "This isn't what I expected either," he said, looking down my bustier. "I thought this was a gay bar."

"It is a gay bar," I said and, displaying my usual grace toward unknown males, shot him a look questioning his sanity. He walked away. "I think I was just hit on," I said to my companions. "Was I hit on?"

"You were hit on," Dave concluded.

"Was he straight?" I asked, incredulous. All I'd noticed was that he looked Hispanic and dressed like a construction worker.

"Straight people come in here all the time," Dave explained, pointing out a biologically boy/girl couple at the neighboring table. To ward off future unwanted advances, Dave hit on the idea of posing as my husband. He demonstrated proper protective husbandly behavior: throwing an arm around my shoulder. Then he remembered what was emblazoned across his T-shirt and splayed his hands across rainbow letters that spelled out "CASTRO STREET."

Ladies' Fetish & Taboo Society
Compendium of Urban Anthropology, 1995

"A restaurant is a fantasy — a kind of living fantasy in which diners are the most important members of the cast."

—WARNER LeRoy

NEW AGE DINING:
SANTA FE

The Planet Cafe glows from its Palace St. storefront, even though the late May sun has not yet set. The distance between the restaurant and the Palace of the Governors is greater than the few physically intervening blocks. An illuminated earth-like hemisphere is mounted on the entrance. Tiny white lights dot the plants and French doors, which are draped with wondrously opalescent, sheer fabric. The menu suggests an investor owns a tofu farm. It is an odd mix of macrobiotic and Thai. I go for macrobiotic. Lasagna sounds challenging.

Like the rest of the customers, I sit outdoors. The interior shines with gorgeous blond wood, but the fresh air is so pleasant. Behind me, three women discuss the romantic woes of one of them. It sounds like her boyfriend is doing something upsetting with her best friend. Details invade my perusal of local give-away newspapers, which meld Native American traditions to New Age nebulousness.

The waiter, who sports an enviously thick ponytail and a heavily affected manner, deposits a tasteless pureed spread and water specked with lemon twists. The older women recommend ditching the boyfriend. At a table to my side, another woman is dictating — addresses, phone numbers, and who was lovers with whom – to a younger woman who appears to be taking notes on the tablecloth itself. The Bay Area figures heavily in the conversation. So does a weird contagious disease.

"In case you get bored," the waiter says, putting a Dixie cup in front of me. I examine the contents: nubby crayons. Their hardness proves that sometimes brand names do make a difference. It's not easy to get much color from these non-Crayolas, but as the waiter predicted, I'm getting bored. The women behind me have left. Self-amusement necessitates drawing a sun, a moon, an intricate pattern of zigzags and circles.

The officious dictating woman drones on. She's coaching the other in the difficult process of coming out, which she went through once and remembers painfully, but of course has moved beyond, since that is no longer her lifestyle.

The waiter apologizes for obscuring my artwork, which has taken on the form of a minor galaxy. I examine the cause of the obscuring. The long-awaited lasagna is an exercise in ingredient substitution. Instead of meat, tofu. Instead of tomato sauce (a previously unsuspected culinary pitfall), carrot and beet puree, which the waiter identifies with considerable glee. Some of it is particularly loathsome.

The tutorial in Lesbianism 101 departs, and some advanced practitioners take the front table. The waiter suggests dessert. He boasts of seven varieties of tofu cheesecake. The concept is overwhelming. I cast my lot with lemon coconut. It is an astonishingly wise choice.

A man, woman, and boy about three take over the table left by the complaining women. A small person toddles out of the restaurant. It has wispy blond hair, clutches a handled bottle, and wobbles as if it is not yet used to movement on this planet. Perhaps this is my first contact with an alien. The being rushes about the courtyard and comes to rest near the family's table, where it squats. A caterwaul immediately erupts from beneath; the son has apparently taken cover and is not happy about being disturbed.

His mother takes charge of the situation. "Now, Michael, George is stressed out. He needs his space." The being identified as Michael runs around to get a closer look at George, who has emerged and retaken his chair. George continues shrieking. The father tries luring Michael into the restaurant. Michael doesn't fall for any of the ploys and yells defensively about his bottle, which he suspects someone is trying to take away. He wants to play with George, or at least let George continue screaming at him. The waiter reappears. "Can't you do something?" the mother asks. "He doesn't respond well to me," the waiter explains. "If I try to talk to him, he'll scream."

Michael runs along the side of the building. A pregnant worker emerges from the restaurant. Despite a strong resemblance to the runaway, she makes no move to contain him. There's nothing for this spectator to do but pay the bill and amble toward the car.

Ladies' Fetish & Taboo Society
Compendium of Urban Anthropology, 1990

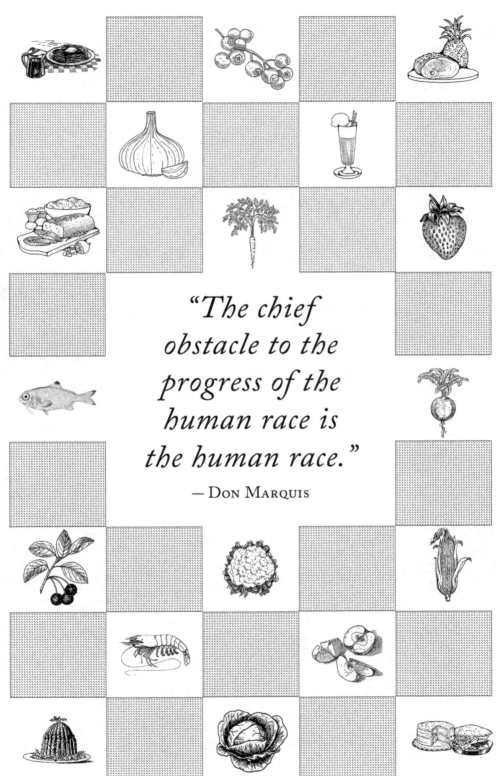

"*The chief obstacle to the progress of the human race is the human race.*"

— Don Marquis

WHEN SERVICE GOES
TO THE DOGS

I don't care how exquisite the food or the surroundings are. A meal will leave a bad aftertaste if the customer walks away feeling mistreated. It's astonishing to me how often this happens – and how easily the ill will could be avoided.

Call me idealistic if you will, but my attitude does have roots in real-world experience. For one thing, I've been on the receiving end of a number of whoppers that turned around spectacularly because of how the staff handled them.

And, just as importantly, I do not come to this topic with the rosy-hued perception that running a restaurant is a breeze. I gained a more-than-vague appreciation of the pressures of this business from a hellish stint at the Dallas restaurant that pioneered the margarita machine. There, during the heyday of the two-for-one happy hour, I got a crash course in coping with mistakes, backstabbing, and flaring tempers — from waiters stealing my orders, to drinks being spilled (as often as not, by me), to customers trying to walk their bill. No matter how badly I wanted to smack my tray onto someone's head, though, I never lost respect for the fact that the ultimate trump card was in the customer's wallet.

This is a concept with astonishingly little currency in my recent experiences on the other side of the table. Now, adult life long ago taught me that common decency is not sufficient reason for some people to treat their fellow mortals as human beings. Neither, apparently, is furthering one's economic self-interest. It certainly hasn't been for a troubling number of servers I've encountered in recent years who've responded in ways that can be most charitably described as self-sabotage, sometimes to provocation no greater than a customer merely existing.

In a decade of reviewing restaurants, I've detected some recurring trends in self-sabotaging service techniques. Interestingly, these have revealed themselves to me only when I was with good-natured, unobtrusive dining companions. None has yet to occur in the presence of a trying personality (believe me, I've dined with a few) that might have triggered, yea perhaps even justified, a particular technique.

At the top of the list is the most frequently occurring tactic, which I like to call...

THE AMAZING DISAPPEARING WAITER

This one rarely rears its mystifying little head before the end of the meal. Come time for the check, though, and poof! Even the most attentive waiter can become inexplicably scarce – at the very moment when it would make most sense to remind the people with the wallet of his or her existence.

That's easily solved, you say; just get the waiter's attention and ask for the check. Sure, that usually works, though it may take a while. (Some people are remarkably impervious to staring, gestures, and other generally accepted signals for attention.)

Assuming your server hasn't vanished, of course. On a dinner visit at Solero early in its incarnation, my buddy and I spent a good 20 minutes gazing toward the kitchen door in the hope of spying our waitress. Not only did she fail to materialize after a meal of perfectly acceptable service, but every other staffer ignored our motions for attention.

Divine bliss was soon to be ours, though. The manager appeared from the other direction and offered to buy us an after-dinner drink, if only we would move to the bar and free up the table. We thanked him and declined, explaining that we really did want to leave and had in fact been trying to get our check for some 30 minutes.

Such satisfaction is rare. (We got our check but fast, by the way, although the waitress never resurfaced.) So is learning the reason behind a disappearing act. When one is revealed, it can be a stunner.

One Houston friend still tells the story of being at lunch at SRO, a trendy Galleria-area spot back in the 1980s, that devolved into a 30-minute  wait for the check. The group finally got the attention of another staffer, who explained that their waiter had been arrested for breaking parole.

I'll concede: The surprise of seeing a staff member carted off by the police might well rattle a manager so badly that no one thinks to reassign the abandoned stations. I have no mercy, though, when the management is not just aware of a problem, but actively contributing to it. This was the case the one time I've received an explanation, and it came after the Amazing Disappearing Waiter act had already sunk the entire meal.

I was in the company of a veteran business luncher, my longtime friend Bill, who is an unfailingly polite person and possesses an excellent rapport with people in the service industry. We were lunching at Teala's, on a first review visit.

That is to say, we were trying to lunch. In the course of 75 minutes, all we got was an appetizer, and that took half an hour to arrive. At least it showed up. In other parts of the restaurant, which was only half full, people were quite obviously eating, but not in our out-of-the-way station, the corner of the main dining room under the stairway. Despite the non-flow of food into our no-man's land, the hostess was continuing to bring newcomers into our increasingly unhappy midst. When one table's order finally did arrive, a neighboring party loudly asked, "How long have you been waiting?"

"An hour and 15 minutes," the answer came back, whereupon a weird camaraderie broke out as the entire room compared notes.

Coincidentally, that was the same length of time that Bill and I rode out this nightmare. Not that we were sitting by sheepishly. He tried three times to alert the management, to no avail. After two visits to the hostess station, he actually walked into the kitchen to find out what was happening to our order. Finally he had to head back to work, so we gave up.

It wasn't until we reached the door that we heard an apology and an explanation. *One of our waiters called in sick … a busboy is taking his place but he's never waited on tables before … of course we'll comp your appetizer and iced tea … you don't want to walk out without eating, do you? We'll be happy to fix you up a bag of fajitas to go … it'll only take a minute.* Which was, alas, a minute more than we had left to invest.

As Johnny Mathis and Deniece Williams croon "Too Much, Too Little, Too Late" off in the distance, let us move to the next technique.

BLAME THE CUSTOMER

Instead of apologizing for or, heaven forbid, fixing a problem, some service people shove responsibility off onto the customer, creating a kind of My-Problem-Is-Your-Problem situation.

Palace Cafe inspired me to come up with the name for this category, when the kitchen was basking in the glory of its first reviews. Bill and I were on another lunch review visit, and this one began precariously. After clearing mashed potatoes from his chair, Bill rested his arm on the window sill, only to discover that his shirt sleeve was dusted with ashes. He was still clearing away his personal space when the waitress joined us.

"His chair's got mashed potatoes in it," I observed. She ignored me.

"Look at this," Bill said, lifting an ash-covered shirt sleeve. "The window sill's all covered with ashes."

"There can't be ashes," she said. "There's no smoking here."

Bill put his arm down on the sill again and lifted it to show her evidence to the contrary.

Her response? "Oh, that's smart, putting your arm back in it." Whereupon she asked for our order. No apology, no towel, no wiping of soiled surfaces.

And then there was the night a friend found an insect in his Scotch at Bayou City Seafood & Pasta. He was drinking his dinner, due to a monumentally bad day at the office, and took this unexpected extra as a further sign that the gods had it in for him.

I encouraged him to tell the waitress. Maybe this was a chance for his day to improve; maybe she's comp a fresh drink. (I'd seen such wonders before. When a roach surfaced in a sandwich in the now long-gone Paradise Bar and Grill, the manager descended in seconds with a hushed apology and comped dessert for our table of eight.)

My companion passed on the news cautiously and gently. The waitress didn't flinch – or apologize. Instead, she disappeared, only to return with a message.

"The bartender says he's not going to open a new bottle," she said.

"I want a bug in my drink," a man announced from a neighboring table. The waitress walked off.

The drink was on the bill.

This phenomenon has an inverse expression as well, more along the lines of Your-Problem-Is-Not-My-Problem. My favorite example took place about 15 years ago, at the first incarnation of Tila's. Late at night, long after the dinner mob had subsided, a friend asked that guacamole be left out of her order of soft chicken tacos because she was allergic to avocado. What she got was abundantly *con* guacamole, so she called the waiter over to repeat her request. The waiter looked irritated but took the plate away. When he placed a plate of tacos in front of her quite a while later, she opened a tortilla just to be sure. It was the very same order with some, but hardly all, of the guacamole scraped away.

These last three servers were mere novices compared to the management of the short-lived Floyd's on Shepherd, which propelled the game of Blame the Customer into unprecedented, public extremes. The problem was shrimp that smelled, well, awful, which I noted in a *Houston Press* Dish column. It ran under the headline "Floyd's and Pseudo-Floyd's," and compared the kitchen that Floyd Landry was actually running while his Cajun Shack was temporarily shuttered for remodeling, with the place on Shepherd that was using his name around the corner from the Shack. (Yes, it's confusing.)

Where's the Blame the Customer in this? In a *Houston Press* ad that followed – and on a portable billboard in front of the restaurant. Both misquoted the column outrageously and played up the only two complimentary adjectives in it: "fine and tasty," which had actually referred to the breading around the smelly shrimp. The ad labeled me a Pseudo-Food Critic, while the billboard used the moniker Pseudo-Food Xpert. (Which quickly went onto my business card. Seriously.)

The ad ran only once, but the billboard stayed, with a new dish going up over my pseudo-endorsement week after week. I waited, figuring that the owner was trying to provoke a response and get tired, sooner or later.

It took a month. Floyd's on Shepherd has since reverted to its former name, Richard Head's, more commonly called Dick Head's.

Before we move on, I must salute the most enigmatic form this multifaceted tactic has taken yet. I phoned the downtown location of Gray's Papaya, a Manhattan hot dog chain that boasts "We Are Polite New Yorkers."

"Are you open 24 hours?" I asked.

"Fuck you!" replied an employee and hung up.

What would he have said if he weren't a polite New Yorker, I wondered.

EVERY CUSTOMER CONTACT IS A POTENTIAL PROFIT CENTER

Of course making sales is a vital aspect of the restaurant business. There is a noticeable distinction between helping customers determine their wishes, though, and pressuring – or outright tricking – them into running up the tab. The first encourages a sense of trust and being cared for. The second makes you feel as if someone's trying to take advantage of you.

My attitude might be more generous-hearted if this behavior coincided with modestly priced menus that were likely to generate paltry tips. I've encountered it, though, only in restaurants that were relatively expensive in the first place.

A waiter at a local steakhouse set off my suspicions early one dinner. After seeing my party of two arrive from the bar with two appetizers already in tow, he took down our order of two steaks and a couple of vegetables, which are served in enormous family-sized portions. Then he recommended that we also split a lobster – which happened to have a market price of $50.[10] When he checked in as we picked at dessert, "May I

bring you anything else?" might have been an appropriate inquiry, but this guy wasn't leaving anything to chance. He asked if we would like a cigar and a Remy Martin. Note the artistry of not just steering us toward an after-dinner drink, instead of mere coffee, but an expensive call liquor.

A waiter at Mandola's Family Table preferred the simple tactic of withholding pertinent information when a girlfriend joined me for my first review visit, at lunch. You may recall that the gimmick at this restaurant was family-sized entrees designed to serve three or four persons. We could have split one and still walked out with a doggie bag. Any wonder that we were aggravated that the waiter let us order two without explaining the concept?

His fib of omission was, of course, immediately obvious. Most padding tactics do come to light by the time the check arrives. (I'm leaving aside the outright fraud of altering the credit card total, which briefly landed a tidy sum for a no-longer-autonomous New York chef, or running a charge through twice, which really happened to a friend of mine in two Houston restaurants.) This is hardly the most self-promoting moment for a waiter to spring a surprise

[10] Note from the future: in 1996 prices.

on customers. I can only guess that someone is banking on the customer not looking very closely at the bill.

Still, even an inattentive customer might pay attention when the bottom line is way out of line with expectations. After I'd already eaten there twice, a very pricey lower Westheimer restaurant broadsided me with an astronomical two-person lunch tab. We'd each ordered the day's special, which had, as is common, been described without any reference to the price. As is also common, I expected specials to cost more than entrees on the menu, which hovered around $15.[11] But nothing prepared me for lunch specials coming in at $30[12] apiece, twice as much as the regular entrees.

I was willing to shoulder blame for the surprise. I should have asked for the price and now I always do. The same restaurant, however, put on charge on a different visit's bill that I had no idea was being incurred. At the waiter's recommendation, I had ordered a bottle of Italian water, but I was charged for two. The waiter's explanation? When the first ran out, he'd replaced it, without bothering to ask. He was adamant. We'd drunk two bottles, however unwittingly, so we had to pay for two bottles. He may have been willing to argue about a handful of dollars in a tab approaching $130,[13] but I wasn't. Besides, it was easier just to adjust the tip.

THE WORSE YOU TREAT SOMEONE, THE MORE THEY LOVE YOU

You know how pop psychologists say women are bored by nice guys and always fall for the ones who treat them badly? There's a definite corollary in the restaurant business. The prime example is an insanely popular Montrose

---

[11] Again from the future: we're talking 1997 prices, which is just under $25 in 2019 terms.

[12] 21st-century me again. That's just under $50 now.

[13] Yo! Just over $200 in 2019 bucks.

institution that couches first-rate food in a crowded, chaotic, body-and-soul pummeling environment.

The din is so all-pervasive that no one gave it a look when a wine-tanked friend stood up and proclaimed her undying love for me. (Not because of the gay-friendly neighborhood, but because nobody had a chance of making out the words.) The waits are so legendary that you'd think no one would ever show up without a reservation, but people still do. In droves.

There's an end to every infatuation, and this experience did it for me.

The ordeal began with getting the table from hell: at the foot of the stairs in a sunken porch that did multiple duty as bar, dining room, and holding tank for customers awaiting tables; in the line of fire of waiters dashing to and from the bar, most of whom allowed us only inches clearance, and many of whom knocked the lone unoccupied chair into the table and into my knees.

Why didn't we ask to move? The place was already full, only 10 minutes after opening – on a Sunday evening. Why didn't we leave? I was on assignment. Sigh.

The waiter registered annoyance when we ordered appetizers. More fools we for not having embraced his desire to hurry us every step of the way. The busboy aborted delivery of our salads after one look at our tabletop, which was crowded by oversized appetizer plates fit for an Edith Ann[14] skit. Our waiter had other priorities; within minutes, he whisked away the appetizers (which were still obviously in progress), switched the plates before we had time to protest, and fled.

By the entree, my companion had spiraled into an animal-instinct irritability, triggered by a relentless stream of people passing within inches of his arm. A throbbing in my throat made me realize we had been shouting to be heard over the blend of synthesizer music, ambient chatter, and intermittent squealing from a neighboring party.

At least we didn't have to wait for the check. It arrived with the desserts.

---

[14] A child that Lily Tomlin played sitting in an oversized chair on the TV show *Laugh-In*.

WHEN SERVICE SHINES

Service doesn't develop (or mutate) in a vacuum. The tone is set by management. When the owners and managers respect their customers and their staff, the probability of good service is greatly enhanced. And with this tight-tight labor market, treating a staff well means more than just adding 50 cents to the hourly wage.

Some restaurateurs offer bonus incentives tied to monthly profits. Some take their best staff to the wine country to taste and learn. Some, such as Edd and Nina Hendee at Taste of Texas, send their entry-level employees to class to learn English and finish high school.

In a perfect world, such courtesies trickle down to the customers. Even a little coddling can make a big difference. Here are a few strategies that can elevate a restaurant visit from merely eating to dining.

Get to know your customers.

A waiter at China Garden used to automatically deliver iced tea and hot and sour soup to a customer who always ordered both. He was secretly thrilled by the attention and was delighted to take friends there.

One of the managers at the now-departed Munchie's won my heart by visibly hovering nearby while I was fending off an obviously unwanted conversation.

Top honors in this category, though, go to a manager at The Woodlands'

Carrabba's, who has fostered a palpable neighborhood atmosphere by greeting regulars by name and then some. When one of the most frequent customers decided to spend his birthday dining alone at the pasta bar, the staff made a point to seat attractive single women next to him.

Thank your customers.

Owner Manfred Jachmich underscored a favorable first impression of The Redwood Grill by visiting with each table one Saturday evening; as my party departed, his staff followed his example with a gauntlet of "Thank yous," from the waitress to the bartender to the hostess.

When a first-time visitor knowledgeably effused about the cooking at the original incarnation of Buttarazzi's, the chef (Aldo el Sharif, before his move inside The Loop), appeared at the table to thank him, then took him on a tour of the kitchen and larder, complete with tastings.

And most remarkably of all, the owners of Cosmos Cafe celebrated their one-year anniversary by giving their customers a party, featuring an enormous and scrumptious dinner – all free – and a dance-inducing band that blazed until the bar closed.

Over the years I've also been witness to spectacular saves from near disasters. Two sure-fire techniques:

I Made a Mistake. I'm Sorry; Let Me Fix It.

When pieces of chopped plastic littered a Jack Daniel pie at the Katy Freeway Saltgrass Steakhouse, the manager didn't just comp my party's desserts, but also explained what had happened (a spatula caught in the mixer) – and thanked us for telling him, so he could pull the damaged pie from the cooler.

I Made a Mistake. I'm Sorry; I've Fixed It.

Finally, nothing beats catching and rectifying a problem before the customer notices that something's wrong. Late one Saturday night at the now-gone Baci, the manager showed up out of the blue with the news that he had comped the table's entrees. He'd discovered that a waiter on another station had swiped a lamb dish earmarked for us. Because it was the last of that particular cut of meat, the manager had taken the liberty of whipping up lamb chops instead, which would be out momentarily. And were.

My Table, 1999

"*Statistics show
that of those who
contract the habit
of eating, very
few survive.*"

— WALLACE IRWIN

139

ALDIWORLD

I enjoy visiting unfamiliar grocery and specialty food stores. I find low-key adventure in wandering the aisles and taking in the product and display choices. At best, the prowling leads to happy-making finds. At worst, it's nothing but a shoulder shrug and a U-turn out the door. But that was before I explored the brave new world of ALDI.

ALDI has had must-visit status for me since a contract German document review job a few years back, when I had heard other lawyer temps rhapsodizing about finding beloved products here on American turf. The chain's from Germany and has been scattershooting outposts across the US. (One of the German owners has a connection now to Trader Joe's as well.) The closest location has been more than an hour away in upstate New York, and the expense of driving that far to visit a discount grocer put the brakes on my curiosity. That came back when I learned that a store had opened only 20 minutes away. (Sit still in Jersey and pretty much every chain will eventually come to you, the past decade has shown me.)

Thanks to vaguely happy memories from Germany and great word of mouth from my informant, I walked in favorably disposed toward ALDI. I expected some of what I encountered: an industrial-to-Spartan layout, no-frills displays of stacked cartons of merchandise, pay-for-push carts, self-bagging. The private labeling was another matter. ALDI doesn't have one label, like A&P's America's Choice or Whole Foods' 365. It has an array of labels with names that create their own discrete universe of marketing altogether, not so much parallel as perpendicular to what otherwise passes for commerce in these United States. Happy Farms milk and cheese. (Cheese was one of the few things I did purchase, and I am perplexed to report that Happy Farms Cheddar Cheese is as close to an extruded block of American cheese as anything I have come across bearing the label "cheddar.") Goldhen eggs. Dakota beans. Tate's mayonnaise and mustard. Cheese Club mac and cheese box mixes. Sea Queen frozen fish (a nod, perhaps to Sea Cuisine in the A&P freezer case?) Aunt Maple's pancake mix and syrup, in fonts and colors that flirt with the trade dress of both Aunt Jemima and Mrs. Butterworth. Fit and Active was the most pervasive brand, cutting across a variety of product types. While I have no problem with those words applied to dried cereal or even yogurt, they are not ones I want to see describing ground turkey; that I want to be anything but active. (I passed up other items in the small butcher case for another reason — the disclosure that they contained enhancers.)

The effort, the deliberateness, the close-but-no-cigar approximation of popular brands were both unsettling and exhausting and triggered a cellular defensiveness that made me physically uncomfortable by the time I rounded the end of the first long aisle. It was a European's carefully crafted but target-missing interpretation of America — like when in the mid-80s I saw the Austrian consul and his wife sporting a zoot suit and *I-Dream-of-Jeannie* hairstyle, respectively, at a Goethe Institute Houston event and a Vietnamese national took issue with my bemusement because they looked exactly as he thought Americans should. ALDI made me feel like I was walking through the IKEA of grocery stores, or a 3D model of a set for a *Simpsons* episode, without that show's intended irony.

I'm sticking to shopping closer to home, geographically and metaphorically speaking.

PS from the future: I've reconciled with ALDI, but only for its organic produce. The branding still weirds me out.

Moon in the 6th, 2010

THE DANGERS
OF MALL-WALKING

I wanted to go for a walk one evening and, for a change, I didn't want to go alone. I suspected my friend David might be game on short notice. To increase the odds, I coached the offer in terms most attractive to him , even though they meant coming into contact with something I normally avoid: going to a mall. I could hear his eyebrows leap at the suggestion. He chose our poison: Sharpstown Mall, an enormous complex on the southwest edge of Houston.

We made it through the ground level without incident. Halfway across the second I spied a maroon-jacketed woman holding a clip board. The marketing researchers were out! I'd been stopped by one, once, more than a decade earlier, in just that spot, I told David, and after freeing myself from her clutches hadn't made it 20 feet before a second had flagged me. "How long has it been since you've taken part in a marketing research study?" he'd asked.

"About 20 seconds," I'd answered. He'd let me off the hook.

The anecdote registered on some level with the maroon-jacketed menace, for soon its latest embodiment was trotting after us. "Ma'am? Ma'am?" she implored, singling me – naturally – out. "Will you take a moment to answer some questions about rice?" I shot a "No, thanks" over my shoulder and kept walking.

We continued our wanderings, exploring every spoke off the main concourse, marveling over the influx of non-Caucasian shops in what had historically been a lily-white stronghold. "Excuse me, ma'am," someone called out. I turned to see a maroon jacket. We quickened our pace.

"Would you be willing to answer some questions about rice?" We kept going. She kept following.

"We'll pay you $20."

I stopped.

Hmmm.

David and I caucused and promptly endorsed the idea. She ushered us into a sparsely furnished reception area, where three or four women were sitting quietly. The minion at the desk handed me a clipboard and a questionnaire that probed my shopping and eating habits. As I checked "no" after "no," my heart glowed at once again skewing a statistical sample.

The researchers had a different reaction. Scanning my answers, one of the maroon-jacketed women paused. "You haven't had any flavored rice in the last three months?"

"No."

"Then you're not eligible to participate," she announced. "Oh, well," I thought and started to leave. "No, we *need* you!" she exclaimed and scurried off to huddle with other minions, who buzzed and counted and conferred. Yet another approached me.

"You haven't had *any* flavored rice in the last three months," she asked, implying it was impossible. Ah, but it wasn't; I shook my head. "No Rice-A-Roni?" I shook my head again. She thought. "Have you eaten in a Chinese restaurant?" I had. "Have you had fried rice?" Yes. "That'll do!" she announced triumphantly. The minions laughed and cheered; one of them announced that we'd be ready to start in a few minutes. I asked if my friend could come along. An apologetic but emphatic no was the reply; whatever this was was only for women. David didn't mind; he has ways of amusing himself in a mall.

The room's distaff population filed down a narrow hallway, lined with doors bearing handwritten KEEP OUT signs and open just enough to show unkempt piles of boxes. Our destination was a room with a round table so big there was barely room to pull a chair out without hitting the wall. A dark TV monitor ate one corner; a man in a tie (but no maroon jacket) stood wearily next to it. A pile of stapled papers and a pencil lay before six chairs. Our host invited us to sit (but not touch the pamphlet!) while we waited for the last participant, a pudgy young woman whose clothing suggested she came closer to skirting the poverty line than anyone else in the room.

He gave us permission to open the handout and instructed us not to turn the page until he said so. The page (and each of its successors) repeated the admonition, as insistently as any public school standardized test. On signal, I flipped to a full page, full color ad for a new variant of Uncle Ben's. At last, an alternative to the tyrannical formula of 1 box rice + 1 flavor packet = 1 dish flavored rice. This new product allows the cook to make less than the entire contents of a box of flavored rice by – here's the novel part – *measuring* the prepackaged flavorings according to the amount of rice used. A series of questions on the next page explored my attitudes about the product, based on the ad. No, no, no, no, no, I checked, down to the last one. Would I buy such a product? There being no box labeled, "Hell, no," I marked the one for "no." So, I noticed, did the pudgy young woman next to me.

Before the next page turn, the door opened and a bevy of staffers entered with blue lunchroom trays, which they placed before us. Each tray held three plastic bowls of yellowish rice, labeled 1, 2, and 3, three plastic spoons, and a paper cup with water. Nobody out front had said anything about having to taste food products. Still, none of us grumbled. In strictly controlled sequence, we were instructed to taste a sample, flip the page, answer a series of questions about appearance, taste, and general desirability, and take a sip of water. The first bowl smacked of chicken liver. The second tasted like unseasoned chicken. The third contained so much salt that the flavor survived multiple sips of water. Between tastings, nobody talked.

The last page called for a ranking, favorite to least and gave a line for explaining first choice. Two was mine; it was a toss-up between the others. I filled in the line with uncharacteristic legibility. "Because it was the least offensive," I wrote.

We had to wait until everyone finished. No one took the opportunity to indulge in a little late-night meal supplementation; every single bowl was scarcely touched. The man thanked us, stressed the importance of what we had just done, and asked if there were any questions. The hand that shot up belonged to the Yuppie among us, whose very appearance signaled West University Place and M.B.A. "What were we tasting?" she asked. "Flavored rice," he answered.

"That's it?" she shot back, appalled at the answer. "That's all we get?"

He nodded. "You mean you're not going to tell us what this stuff was?!" she pressed. "Was this Uncle Ben's?"

He didn't know. "All we're told," he admitted, "Is that it's flavored rice."

Unified by let-down, we broke out in chatter at last as we filed out to claim our checks. The woman behind me, whose appearance straddled the line between East Texas and 70s throwback, asked what my first choice was. "That was mine, too!" she exclaimed and asked for my reason. It cracked her up. She never buys this kind of product either. Similar confessions wafted down the hallway as I advanced on recompense, the mall, and the eventual reuniting with my friend.

Ladies' Fetish & Taboo Society
Compendium of Urban Anthropology, 1998

"*But when the time comes that a man has had his dinner, then the true man comes to the surface.*"

— MARK TWAIN

MIDSUMMER MAGIC

Puddle jumping was not what I had in mind for this past summer. Spending just about every non-working hour singing and dancing and praising Jesus was far more likely[15] – especially after I got called back for the role of Mary in a production of *Jesus Christ Superstar*. But that was before the phone rang, between auditions, summoning me[16] to England for an all-night, black-tie, Solstice-tide party on an estate in Dorset.

The messenger was my longest-time friend Hugh. A year ago, he'd issued a deadline of December '94 for a return trip to the island, so we could indulge in one of his pet extravagances – having dinner and champagne catered at a box at the Royal Opera House – before it closes for renovation. This prospect truncated the time frame considerably. It would be the party of the decade, argued Hugh, in terms that threatened consequences for nonattendance.

Scheduling obstacles evaporated with final auditions that night.[17]

---

[15] Fear not, gentle and devoted readers, that the impetus was a religious conversion-cum-personality change. I just wanted to lodge a mainstream theatrical credit onto the performance resume.

[16] "Haul your ass over here" was, if I recall correctly, the exact nature of the command.

[17] I knew, as soon as I sang her song on their stage, that I was not this production's Mary. A place in the chorus, on the other hand, felt like a sure thing. Either my sensors were off, or the invitation marked one of those weird moments when the course of events jumps track from one possible future to another. I didn't make the cast, but a woman did who'd sung an entire verse of "Don't Cry For Me Argentina" under pitch. The appropriateness of this usually undesirable talent did not become apparent until I actually saw the production.

Financial obstacles evaporated with an invitation to stay at Hugh's flat, followed by frequent invocations of that all-American mantra, "Charge it!" Sartorial obstacles evaporated when gay men got wind of them and indulged their gender-based prerogative for fixing things. A member of the Gay Men's Chorus of Houston lent one of his stage dresses,[18] while a client mapped out the drag queen

trail to a neighborhood of warehouses teeming with Indian beaded gowns sized to hug a spectrum of body shapes.

The dresses made me feel like a cross between the Spider Woman and Barbie in the va-va-voom evening gown that came with a microphone. "Not flashy! Not flashy!" the sales clerk insisted as light splintered off sequins and bugle beads, but no matter how much an integral element of Lone Star black tie, a beaded Amazonian breastplate hardly seemed a safe bet for Britain. I settled on a simple black gown and a gold-and-silver sequined jacket – which still ended up wildly overshooting the glitz parameters set by the rest of the partygoers.

Exactly what I was doing with an invitation is a bit convoluted.[19] Hugh has been friends with the hosts, Harold and Tess, since he and Harold worked for the Paris branch of Chase Manhattan Bank.[20] I met them in Barcelona, at a celebration of Hugh's that now has historic effect only, and spent an afternoon with them wandering around various phantasms created by Antonin Gaudi.

---

[18] The size was right, the shape even flattering, the concept perversely appealing.

[19] No precedent here!

[20] For those of you just joining this monologue, Hugh has been my friend since fourth grade.

Our contact has since been in the form of Christmas cards and snippets of news passed through our mutual friend. When Hugh called with this invitation, a memory flashed of Tess describing a marvelous fancy dress party they'd thrown around Midsummer. (I remember this not just because of the content, but also the backdrop, a particularly fantastical, angel-laden area of Gaudi's unfinished cathedral Sagrada Familia in Barcelona.) "How could you not go?" was the universal[21] reaction to the prospect. By the time a printed invitation arrived with Harold's handwritten urging to make a special trip, I had a definitive answer to that question.

Immigration Official: What is the purpose of your trip?

Arriving Passenger: Total frivolity.

"You didn't come all the way from America to go to a party," exclaimed the politely incredulous taxi driver.

"Why, as a matter of fact, I did," I got to respond, one of the most satisfying outlandish but true utterances of a life full of so many.

It didn't take long to get out of town and enter an expanse of rolling green hills, of the sort that inspires bad poetry, futile photo snapping, and pangs of longing. We drove into a descending tunnel of vegetation, a lane wide enough for only one car, with a high wall on the left, hedges on the right, and growth all around so thick that it blocked out the sky.

The driver said his mobile phone loses its reception in the valley this road dips into. I liked him; he said his wife worked at the hotel and his passion was golf. He placed my Texas home on his internal map by its proximity to renowned golf courses and tournaments.

The narrow lane opened onto a curving road with tiny houses huddled up against it. "This is what you would call 'quaint village life,'" he laughed. The sign for the estate was so innocuous that the driver passed it and had to turn

---

[21] Even my mother's.

around by a farm building. The one-lane road inside the gateway, easily half a mile long, was lined with lit torches. The dim light of the setting sun cast a haze over the rectangular box of a house off in the distance. "I feel like I'm in a Merchant Ivory production," I said.

For the next seven hours I wandered like an extra without a director. The hosts had gone to the trouble of printing a schedule of refreshments

and diversions that would take place across the grounds from 9:30 p.m. - 4:46[22] a.m. Champagne, elderflower wine, and hors d'oeuvres in the main house. Seafood and white wine, woodwinds, a sitar, didgeridoo, and fire jugglers at the grotto.[23] Boogie-woogie piano, Dixieland jazz, tap dancing, New Orleans-style drink service,[24] and a Caribbean grill at the pool house.[25] Swing, then blues, then ska bands in a tent alongside the house. French cheese, 1974 Pauillac, kid, lamb, and goat in the wild garden. Desserts and coffees in the pool house; sorbets and crepes at the north end of the pool. Radio-controlled car racing on the tennis courts (1:15 - 3 a.m.).[26] Billiards, fresh fruit buffet, and harp in the house. Coffee, croissants, and ceilidh dancing at dawn on the sunken lawn.[27]

---

[22] Sunrise.

[23] Be still, my heart!

[24] Rum punch, virgin piña coladas, mint juleps, and so-called margaritas, the appearance of which prompted a loud "I don't think so" from these lips – and I wasn't anywhere near drunk.

[25] Well, to be exact, the tap dancer was actually *in* the drained pool.

[26] Which turned out not to be particularly interesting. About half the cars were out of commission, despite the efforts of two teenagers who had the job of maintenance, repair, and battery checks.

[27] One person aptly compared it to taking 300 people to 30 different night clubs. It was a rare convergence of a massive outlay of money (which must have exceeded my taxable income for last year) and exquisite taste. Not one bite of the food was a caterer's filler, nor at all representative of the reputation of British cuisine.

Since the schedule did not reach my hands for several hours, I explored the grounds with no preconception of what was about to take place there. It was set for magic. Behind the house was a sunken lawn, delineated in the equivalent of rooms by high walls of immaculately trimmed hedges. Wide breaks in the growth served as doorways. Against the greenery stood tall chunks of Styrofoam, floodlit from below, that had been whittled away to suggest female figures in motion. Pairs served as gatekeepers on each side of the opening onto a wide expanse that led to the small pavilion tents with cocktail tables and beyond them, a small semi-circular stone structure lined with columns, called the grotto. Inside were tiny, twinkling white lights, a tumbling waterfall that bordered on garish, surrounded by green plants, and two stands that crossed over into garish, covered with nets and sea shells. The air was cool enough for a jacket; the sky was clear. Magical passageways, one canopied and lined with tiny sculptures lit from above, stretched out through the hedges to settings adorned with lights and exotic plants. Birds of paradise[28] encircled a small, round, drained pool beneath a colonnaded rotunda; beyond the next stand of trees, a large pavilion, walls lined with more twinkling white lights, extended one wing of the house. A femalesque Styrofoam figure reclined along an outdoor pool; dramatically angled floodlights accentuated the weirdly varied colors of the vegetation – shades of browns and greens – which reflected in the water.

[28] In pots. Not just growing, but flourishing.

Unprecedented photo opportunities abounded, and many of the guests, which numbered around 300, had also come prepared to take advantage of the sights. Astonishment proved to be a universal language. It was comforting to watch the well-heeled and Oxbridge-accented stop in their tracks, go slack-jawed at some breath-taking detail of the grounds and put their cameras to work.

Your mission, should you choose to accept it, is to impersonate a rich Texan.

My first conversation took place on the front steps of the house, with a man possessed by a concern that arriving guests would mistake us for Harold and Tess. "Not after they hear me," I replied the first time he voiced it. The news that I'm from Texas prompted him to bring up Howard Baker, whom he mistakenly thought had been a senator from that state, and repeat an anecdote about John Connally telling Baker that he saw the president get hit and heard him cry out before being hit himself, which convinced Connally that two shots had been fired. Once again, the mere name of my state of residence triggered a JFK assassination story, but the preamble was so disconcerting that I hadn't seen the cliché coming. An exit cue immediately followed, when the

fear resurfaced about our being confused for the hosts.

I saw the man who would not be Harold once more, playing French horn in a woodwind quintet outside the grotto, while people pushed their way inside for crab salad and salmon and sushi. "It's a fairyland, isn't it?" said a woman with shaggy long hair, wild eyes and a long knit dress that gave modest testimony to how often she traveled in these circles. (The attire was varied – Harold wore swallowtails, Tess changed her gown and let her hair down mid-party, and sensible walking sandals peeked out from many a long skirt – but in the dark, and in this environment, no one looked much.)

Caroline was a violist and mother of six who'd driven in from Cornwall, which she called a savage landscape that takes hold of people so they never leave; she was a friend of Tess' since their teen years and one of the few guests actually staying in the house. She was waiting for his sister Julia, who turned up soon with a tiny infant named Henry strapped in a papoose across her evening gown. Throughout the night, Caroline and Julia met up with me again and again, reappearing and vanishing as if moving through dimensions.

I met another childhood girlfriend of Tess' who had come to the party with a sister, when two couples in line for kebabs drew me briefly into conversation. The husband of one was an American composer who'd been living in London and had been on sabbatical in Austin; it turned out that – what else? – we'd lived in the same neighborhood in that city. He introduced a management consultant, who was the only person to trap me into a conversation about business, although I overheard several of the same involving indefatigably networking Hugh. In the straw-strewn wild garden pavilion, I met a banker from New Orleans, whose husband had gone to Cambridge with Harold and had abandoned law for media consultancy, Republican-style, and an anthropologist working in the Philippines. The award for farthest distance traveled went to none of us, but to yet another of Tess' childhood friends, who'd flown in from China.

After four or five glasses of champagne, a rum punch (the virgin piña coladas had run out), and a glass of wine, I opted for solid sugars in the pool house dessert spread. I lined up between two talkative and friendly younger men who said they were in the ska band. One, in a 50s-style suit and pompadour, insisted on giving me a taste of what must be the dessert of the moment, tiramisu. His less talkative friend wore little more than a high-rise mohawk.

At one point, I rested in a chair, beneath the branches of a ring of trees, next to a small, contained fire; the heels of my shoes had become ruined by sinking into the turf so often, and those of my feet were pulsating with overuse. At another, I was back in the house in one of the side rooms, wallpapered with a Chinese scene, where a woman played the Irish harp and an extravagant mound of fresh fruit spilled onto the table. The tableaux reminded me of a Peter Greenaway film. To me, it felt as festive as Christmas.

The ska band was the only entertainment that quelled my *wanderlust*. The Trojans[29] were a huge crew, six or seven men, some white, some in dreadlocks. The pompadour was the drummer; the mohawk was the vocalist. He and a few others wore torso armor; the barefoot singer wore little else, brandished an enormous spear and jumped incessantly from one leg to the other. High energy and very tight, they put a ska bass and rhythm to all sorts of music – Celtic, Russian, "Scotland the Brave" bleated on bagpipe, which got even old people flailing on the dance floor. "We're going till dawn!" Mr. Mohawk

---

[29] Leads on locating any of the four CDs recorded by this London-based band are hereby solicited. No store I checked stocked them.

exclaimed, but Harold thwarted this intention by shutting them down 30 minutes after their set was supposed to have ended.

The final band, not to mention piles and piles of croissants, were waiting behind the house. Three groups of couples formed to dance a reel, stumble, and break into laughter. The sky was turning pink with the rising sun. I took my leave of Caroline and Julia and headed for a line of taxis outside the freestanding arch at the head of the drive. As we drove off, an angelic opera chorus was playing on the radio.

Ladies' Fetish & Taboo Society
Compendium of Urban Anthropology, 1994

"*You must be careful about giving any drink whatsoever to a bore. A lit-up bore is the worst in the world.*"

— DAVID CECIL

THE OMNI-DIRECTIONAL
SCUD LUST MISSILE REARS
ITS UNWELCOME HEAD AGAIN
AND THIS TIME, SHE'S BROUGHT A FRIEND

The Place: Athens Bar & Grill, which draws an uneasy mix of families, home-town tourists nostalgic for those long-gone days when the kitchen was skilled, Greek sailors who've come ashore from the nearby Ship Channel for an evening of whatever, and women who might oblige – a steaming cocktail of sight-seeing and real danger.

The Time: The eve of Greek Easter, promised to be a hopping time due to the anticipated presence of large numbers of the first and third components of the mix.

The Excuse: Some friends have a client who has a friend who'll be bellydancing that night. My friends are massage therapists Melinda and Jana, who is appearing for the evening in her Madam Ya-Ya persona (which involves rhinestone-studded bat-wing glasses and cigarette holder, a Cramps t-shirt, and an I-Dare-You-To-Say-Something-To-Me air). Why they have talked me into coming along, and why I have capitulated, is that I have been, uncharacteristically, very, very bored.

The band is in full swing when we walk in. It's shrunk as much as an oil company's geology staff since my last visit more than a decade ago. It's now down to three: a balalaika, a female vocalist in a tight evening gown, and a Roland organ. The organ has replaced the drums, lead guitar, and bass. Its treble will double the balalaika in every song throughout the evening, but there's no suggestion of supplanting that instrument as well; the balalaika player's prima donna status ensures job security.

The party we're joining consists of 12 to 14 non-Greeks at the biggest table in the place, including: the evening's belly dancer, decked out in pre-performance white suit with bugle-beaded bustier. An urban shaman (middle-aged, WASP, perpetually grinning, introduced to me as the man who cast negative energy out of a friend's place of business), his daughter, and his wife, who will not crack a smile all evening. A couple I know: Linda, who used to dance there, and her boyfriend.[30] Two long-haired, slender women in spaghetti-strap tank tops and jeans: Ms. X, who is The Client (see "The Excuse," above), and Ms. Y.[31]

I am seated to the right of Ms. X and Ms. Y, next to Melinda, who is at the end of the table, and across from Ya-Ya. Just where this evening is headed is signaled at the outset, when Ms. Y greets us with conversational volleys directed at Melinda ("Where do I know you from? Come on – tell me!!") and, recognizing no impediment in my presence, leans into me to enhance her vantage point. The invasion is auric only; although I feel knocked several feet to the right, my entire body is still firmly on the chair, a disquieting sensation that will continue for the next few hours. A squeal of "What sign are you?" erupts in the vicinity of Mss. X and Y. "I'm a Capricorn, what are you?" Ms. Y gushes at Melinda. "My sign is KEEP OUT," I interject. No one reacts; my voice is as imperceptible as my body. I have achieved fly-on-the-wall status,

---

[30] Who prefers to remain nameless, in these pages, at least.

[31] Linda's boyfriend suggested calling them "Madame Y and Madame Y Not?" but the names could apply interchangeably, and we wouldn't want to confuse you.

which soon proves to be the only safe perspective.

Although she is not the evening's belly dancer, Linda does take the stage to perform graceful, solemn Greek dances learned during her previous tenure. Other patrons join in, or throw dollar bills onto the dance floor (which are swept up for the band), and everything is fine until the line dances disintegrate into slow, free-form gyrating, which Mss. X and Y treat as an invitation to take their act center stage.

When not dancing with Ms. Y, Ms. X monopolizes the Shaman on the dance floor, while his wife languishes at the table or dances alone. Both Mss. make repeated, unsuccessful attempts to lure Ya-Ya and Melinda onto the floor. Ms. Y keeps throwing her body across Melinda's seated torso, a position that makes it all the easier for Ya-Ya to sprinkle salt on bare shoulders at close range. ("That's how you get rid of a slug, isn't it?" she justifies.)

Back at the table, Ms. X stands up, unzips her jeans, and pulls them apart to expose her underwear.[32] She tries to poll the group about how many of us have had sweet "sticks," only no one but her cares to disclose any information (two, she says, and they were sweet as honey). After a set of swirling, candelabra balancing, and engulfing men in her scarves while they tuck cash into her bounteous cleavage,[33] the belly dancer declines to return to our table.

When Linda's boyfriend exits to smoke a cigarette, I retreat to the opposite side of the table, which leaves a vacant seat next to the Mss. When he returns, Ms. Y takes the opportunity to slide her leg between his. The Mss. drape themselves simultaneously around his shoulders. Ms. X bobs her head up and down over his lap until he realizes what she's simulating[34] and pushes her away. Ms. X also plunges her hand down the blouse of a woman with

---

[32] By this time, the table behind her has been occupied by Greek sailors.

[33] "If Madame Ya-Ya were a bellydancer she'd wear a change machine!" Ya-Ya cackled and sketched out the concept on a napkin.

[34] See footnote 32.

known bisexual tendencies and a far greater sense of propriety, who deflects the assault with the warning, "Don't do that or I'll take you up on it." Ms. X, uncharacteristically, retreats.

The lights go out; it's Easter. Waitresses deliver baskets of what look like Roma tomatoes. They're dyed red eggs. Each of us is supposed to take one and tap an end against another person's until the eggs crack. All over the restaurant people are actually butting eggs together, from the balalaika player and the singer, to everyone at our table. Ya-Ya ends up with a piece shaped like a contact lens, which she puts over her eyes. To emphasize the point, she takes it off and inks on an eyeball. "You know what the logical extension is," I say to Ya-Ya, and damned if Ms. X isn't already doing it: Giggling, she's proudly balancing two eggs tips on her chest that are just about the height of the breasts they're covering. "You know she's the person who's making the video on how to give a blow job, don't you?" Ya-Ya reminds me. This I hadn't heard about, but several anecdotes of recklessness she's told me at different times race through my mind and coalesce into one person, who happens to be sitting across from me.

The Mss. retire, together, to the restroom. When nature forces Melinda to follow against her better judgment, she walks in on them hugging against the wall. They link up for all to see during the next slow, gyrating free-for-all on the dance floor. As if no one could have missed what they've been up to, they stand crotch to buttocks and shimmy to the floor and back repeatedly. "It looks like a Grade D lesbian movie," Ya-Ya moans. Linda returns to the table and announces that she can't go up there again, because it's getting too nasty. She reports that the balalaika player pulled her over to the side and barked, "Those women are lesbians!"

Families start arriving wearing church best and holding candles; services must be out. It's a signal. Ya-Ya, Melinda, and I get out while we can. Ms. X is thrown out of the place, finally, after engaging the management in a screaming match which moves from the dining room into the kitchen, over a $1 dispute about the tax on her bill.

Ladies' Fetish & Taboo Society
Compendium of Urban Anthropology, 1994

> *"Elegance
> is the art of not
> astonishing."*
>
> — JEAN COCTEAU

NIGHTCLUB HELL

I t's not the sort of place you ever intend to go to. You never have any
inkling that you're entering it, and once you're there your increasingly
insistent priority is getting out. It crops up unexpectedly, unwelcomely, in
highly unlikely times and places. It is undetectable and unrecognizable until
you've been sucked into the middle of it, surrounded by rapidly encroaching,
dumbfounding – well, hell.

It has no warning signs. None of the usual irritants – poor ventilation, overly
ambitious sound system, drunken patrons, attitude-ridden staff, expensive but
awful libations – are indicative of Nightclub Hell. In fact, all are strangely
absent.

Nothing, it seems, gives any clue that you're in for an experience that will
test your ability to ride herd on your spontaneous and subconscious reactions...
until the entertainment begins. And that is the low, low, lowest common
denominator, the single indicator of hell with a liquor license.

Just what am I rambling on about this time? Read further only if you dare.
Even a vicarious brush can be difficult.

I discovered the existence of this outpost of the nether regions in the fall of
1985, during a convention in San Antonio of Texas Monthly restaurant and
nightclub listers. After hours of speeches and a meal punctuated by nitpicking
criticism by chronically dissatisfied restaurant writers, several of us set out

on foot from our Alamo-neighboring hotel in search of more light-hearted entertainment. The Dallas bar-lister broke from the ranks quite quickly, because, as he boasted, he had rented a car and was on the lookout for really cool jazz.

The rest of us trudged from one dreary hotel bar to another, the only thing to recommend them being proximity, till someone thought of the bar at the Menger Hotel where Teddy Roosevelt recruited Rough Riders. The group trundled over and pressed its collective noses against the glass door. It was only 9 p.m. on Saturday, but the bar was dark and locked.

Someone ferreted out another bar at the end of a corridor. The air felt like vaporizer mist. It reminded me of the suffocating scents at the old Melrose Hotel in Dallas, which I'd breathed unwillingly when my high school choir dropped by the senior citizens' hostelry to sing Christmas programs at Rotary Club luncheons. The similarity was not a coincidence. All of the clientele consisted of white-haired elderly couples and a few strangely familiar but not entirely enthusiastic representatives of the young middle-aged.

Well, well, well. There sat the Dallas bar-lister, alone at a table, while his girlfriend touch-danced with his counterpart from Fort Worth. Far from the sought-for cool jazz, the music came from a blind man who was playing swell chords on a keyboard (left hand) and melodies on a piano (right hand) and soon augmented his chording with a recitation of "How Do I Love Thee? Let Me Count The Ways." He also talked a lot about being in the area of various cities in Washington state, even though we were in San Antonio, Texas.

Two years of being paid to spend time in bars had not put me in contact with anything like this. Tipped off to our presence, the pianist effusively complimented the magazine's recordings for the blind. When he directed birthday greetings to a member of our party (whose birthday it most definitely was not – some cruel jokester had obviously plied him with misinformation) and broke into the most frequently performed song of modern times, my ability to maintain composure was spent. I had to leave.

My second visit to Nightclub Hell did not include such a safe and handy escape route. Extreme hours, language barriers, and a complete lack of any earthly idea where I was were just a few of the incentives for staying put.

This excursion was the aftermath of a rehearsal dinner that had begun at 10:30 p.m., a continental hour consistent with its location in a posh section of Barcelona, Spain. The wedding couple and a small group of friends from various countries headed into the night to continue the party. After all, it was only 1 or so, and several hours remained until daylight. Following the suggestion of another American (who would later be twice permitted by my hotel staff – my phone had been broken since check-in – to attack my door during the night in search of the full names and hotel of the people in whose presence

he had last seen his passport, and whose continued good health and mobility depends on his never entering my sight again), we disembarked from taxis in a narrow, seedy alley and piled into a little cabaret.

Covered with glossy photographs of 20-year-earlier versions of people who later took the stage, La Bodega was a hotbed of has-been performers who, not always wisely, did not let age dim their flamboyance and desire to sing. There were perhaps two or three clusters of patrons in the tiny auditorium-style seating; one was, inexplicably, a pair of extremely punkish young women.

When we walked in, a man was standing on the stage with his back to us and pressing a control on a small portable cassette player. His singing along with the tape provided our introduction to La Bodega's peculiar entertainment. Following him was a woman who displayed the most successful deadlock on innate attractiveness and talent and sang "Valencia-ah-ah-ah" while banging a microphone against her thigh.

Her surreal successor sported a golden-days Lucille Ball make-up job, with eyelashes attached and brows drawn in such a way that it was hard to locate her eyes exactly. She provided her own fanfare while jumping onto the stage and then lifted her plain shirtdress in a gratuitous display of, fortunately, run-of-the-mill briefs. Excessive hand motions characterized her song, which my friend, the groom and my former grade-school cello stand partner, translated as a lamenting of the passing of a little child named Joey.

About this time he also began pressing me to take the stage myself, which prompted me to warn him that he'd better shut up or I'd break his fucking finger (in my first ever enunciation of that particular modifier) and twisted the finger in question menacingly. Another man with a semblance of talent and panache gave her a break, but Our Lady of Gesticulation was soon back, having been informed of the presence of our group. In our honor she chose to sing a song by an American great, "Elvish Preshley." Identifying the song was difficult, though, because the diction sounded like a bizarre vowel shift was occurring right before us: "Eeeez now are nayver [arms outstretched beseechingly], luff mee toonaht [hands over heart], hole me mah darrrlieeng [self-hug], bee mahn toonaht [hands fluttering in an incongruous series of tiny waves toward stage right]."

Even this establishment had its limit, though, and shut down at 2 a.m., sending us back out into the streets in search of a pair of taxis. As we were carried away in the just-before-the-dawn's-early light, the bride leaned out her taxi's window and serenaded her groom, speeding along beside her in the next lane, "eeees now are nayvuh..."

Nightclub Hell reared its offensive head once again last spring, as usual in most unlikely circumstances: the middle of the day in Madrid (emphasis on the first syllable to you), New Mexico, a one-time mining town and overgrown hippie commune.

A cold beer sounded good to one of my traveling companions, so we went into the Mine Shaft Tavern – just after 2 p.m. with the sun blazing overhead unimpeded by clouds. The dark bar had mural panels of trains and snow on miners' cabins; overall the feel was old, old West.

Partway into our order of chips and a burger, a woman took the stage. She looked to be a contender for charter membership in the commune. Her long, straight greying hair was pulled back in a clip; a Chivas Regal bag hung from her belt. She began playing the lick from "Freight Train," which she then sang in a slight, wobbly voice. Polite applause broke out from a few portions of the room. The next chord progression sounded like "The Night They Drove Old Dixie Down," minus the bass run. It was. "House Of the Rising Sun" sent the audience's attention back to conversing. Only two tables applauded. My friend predicted that the next song would be "Me and Bobby McGee." I thought it was too recent, but I was soon proven wrong.

After "Fire and Rain," I was the only person keeping up the pretense of politeness and applauding. "I Can See Clearly Now' caused me to break out in a grin of disbelief so hard to suppress that the bathroom seemed a safer place than our table, which was the closest to the stage. The next chord progression sounded like – no – it was, really – the killer hit from that proto-soft rock group Bread, "If." I found myself standing in line in an aging building's restroom listening to music from my sophomore year in high school and focusing on a stall door with a jagged piece cut out so it could clear the toilet. Once behind the door myself, I heard the beginning strains of "Wichita Lineman." Had no sheet music reached this place since the early 1970s?

I didn't have to talk my friends into running for it. We ambled through the few shops along the town's rocky, dusty street – wondered who could pay $1200 for a kimono jacket, listened to a leather-jacketed, motorcycle-riding boy scream "fuck!" every other word, watched the llama cart go by (rides $1; "things you can do with a llama: riding – packing – companionship & pet"), stumbled across some Afghan pilgrims' jewelry containing prayers – and as we got into the car, recognized the strains of "Long Black Veil" floating out of the Mine Shaft Tavern. The question was, did she learn it from the Grateful Dead or from the Joan Baez songbook?

And the moral of the story? Two, possibly. Contrary to what your mother always told you, it may actually be safer to go to bars alone than in groups. And run for it – or be prepared to endure the consequences – at the first sign that entertainment is aware of your group's distinguishing characteristics.

Ladies' Fetish & Taboo Society
Compendium of Urban Anthropology, 1990

*"Gourmet:
Usually little more
than a glutton
festooned with
credit cards."*

— SYDNEY HARRIS

ZEITGEIST: THUMBNOSING
(WHOOPEE! WE'RE ALL GONNA DIE)

This essay contains an unexpurgated rant that appeared in shortened form in "When Service Goes To the Dogs."

It started with the coffee bars, which have sprung up across the nation as if scattered from the windblown head of some dandelion in Seattle. Four years ago, iced coffee was nowhere to be found even in the hippest, hottest part of Houston, a lack that only fueled the disdain of rabble-rousers who flew in from NYC to disrupt the Republican National Convention. Now the brew of the bean is available any which way just about anywhere (except, so far, in a parking lot kiosk or a drive-through) all over the city.

Locally owned, single-location bars formed the advance guard, followed quickly, before loyalties solidified, by national chains. (The entry of Starbucks and Brothers prompted one of the first claim-stakers to outfit its employees in t-shirts with the slogan on the back "Corporate Coffee Sucks.") A common denominator binds all these uppity purveyors: what they serve is a damned sight better than the bitter joe that comes out of the machines at, say, McDonald's.[35] Those of us who once tolerated coffee for the jump-start

---

[35] Which, by the way, has put stickers on its drive-through windows warning customers about the potentially scalding temperature of coffee.

are now slurping down its multifaceted variations for the taste. This vehicle for high-octane caffeine is seriously challenging the status of iced tea as all-season default drink.[36]

Next came the dark cloud of cigar smoke, first in the backrooms of nightclubs and gradually billowing out across the public scene. As if to counterweight the plummet in number of places permitting smoking, cigar bars are flourishing with a vengeance, adding an air of pretension (and outright stench) to tattered coffeehouses and tony restaurants alike. It's not just a male clientele that has proven willing to shell out more for a tobacco consumable than for a drink spiked with call liquor; women-only societies and fundraisers have sprung up centering around this puffing pastime. At stake is more than the opportunity of getting wired, which caffeine, quietly, provides. Cigars make a public statement, and a public impact. Maybe the smoker doesn't inhale, but everyone around him certainly does.

And all the while, King Cattle has been horning its way back into the hearts and bellies of diners. In the last few years, concerns of health consciousness have spilled over from private kitchens to restaurant menus, which have given

greater play to chicken, fish, and (don't look now, but even in Texas) meat-free menus. But beef never went away; it's been biding its time, working its way back into our appetites to a soundtrack from Coupland's "Rodeo," waiting for those moments that demand something juicy, bloody, and red. Their time returning, steaks are reappearing on the menus of new, trendy, decidedly upscale operations that target an audience with an

[36] Fifteen years ago a Texan I knew, on his first business trip to Canada, ordered iced tea in February. The waitress screamed.

education and disposable income, or at least untapped-out lines of credit. And dominance isn't being reclaimed by dainty little filets, either, but by hefty cuts that weigh in well over a pound, more animal protein than a body needs in a day, much less a meal.

All this quaffing and puffing and fat-chewing have a low common denominator indeed: Each is a brazen, public defiance of What's Good For You. It's recklessly retro, this deliberate consumption of substances now known to be potent with danger. But it feels like more than a backlash against the health-promoting limitations that are permeating our culture. On a deep level, what this phenomenon is really targeting is the future. Caffeine and cigars and cows are converging in one collective outcry of pre-millennial angst.

Ground zero for the primal scream is a newish restaurant in Houston that is basing its fortune on consuming as if tomorrow will never come. The family owners, who have spent decades applying the concept of reliable, decently priced cooking to a variety of ethnicities, have decided to leap upscale with a steakhouse. They've left behind traits that won customer loyalty and adopted characteristics fraught with the anxiety that someone might, somehow, fail to catch the metamorphosis. With the finesse of Americans in 1940s movies, they've printed big bold words across the awning announcing "fine wines" and "vintage cigars" and coached their employees to bring home, at every turn, just how high-falutin' this place is. True, it is full of gorgeously mid-century touches (stylized fonts, gold foil logos on glass, period lamps, railroad dining car seating fit for an Agatha Christie mystery), creating a luscious illusion of going back in time. But it's the beauty of the adage, and what lies beneath the surface here skims it as well. From the seating policy to huckster waiters to prices that slack the jaw of a veteran business account diner, this place traffics in audacity and pretension. And folks are responding to the ploy by spending with an abandon that's been laying low since the Me Decade gave way to the Why Me?

Business reasons took me into this time warp, and not even they could lure me in again. The experiences of one visit so upset me that I could barely focus my mind on work the next morning.

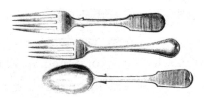

Arriving without reservations at 7 p.m. on a Thursday, my party was given an estimate of up to an hour and a half for a seat.[37] (If we had made reservations, we would have been required to call 3-7 days in advance,[38] and even then would have been warned to expect a 15-30 minute delay. Yup; with reservations.) Morbidly curious about what could be worth such a wait, we settled in at the piano in the ranch-rustic lounge, where clusters of men sucked on cigars underneath enormous circular vents. Strangely, artificial rose, and not smoke, was the prevailing scent, and no smell at all emanated from the floral arrangement that propped up the piece of cardstock on which the hostess had written our party's name. This low-tech element was the pivot point of a bizarre match game, in which hostesses silently held up cardstock lettered with a surname as they walked through the lounge and looked for its mate. Before ours showed up, the bar waitress delivered our first shock of the evening (the cheerfully delivered news that per-glass wine prices began at $7[39]) and menus, which provided the second. Entrees started at $20[40] for a

---

[37] Note from the future: this New York-style delay was utterly unprecedented in Houston at this time.

[38] Ditto, and ditto.

[39] Ditto, more than $13 in 2019 and nearly twice what I was used to.

[40] Nearly $40 now.

cut of steak, prime rib, lamb or veal; one fish and two lobster dishes were the only deviations from red meat; and vegetables were extra, offered "family style" for $3-$8.[41] From then on, shock after shock detonated throughout the meal.

Appetizers were on their way out of the kitchen when a hostess brandished our name in the lounge. They followed us to the table, where they lay in plain view while the waiter suggested that we split a lobster ($48.95 for 20 ounces) as an appetizer. He also handed over a wine list with scarcely a bottle under $100, most over $300 and one for $10,000. He took it calmly when we ordered only house salads, two steaks, and a couple of vegetables.

What we got was an exercise in maximizing fat content. Even the salad was topped with cheese and bacon, which also littered the mashed potatoes. Everything but the salad was dripping with butter and left a film like an oil slick on the palate. The biggest disappointment was the main course; the steaks, which the waiter had touted as the best in town, were charred and unevenly textured, a mishandling that should have caused any self-respecting Texan to take offense.

Nobody but us seemed to mind. All around were men in suits, loosened ties, and Rolexes, talking bidness and indulging in a rampant extravagance

---

[41] $6-15 in 2019.

that brought to mind blow-out recruiting dinners of the early 80s (and, as my cynicism progressed, the final days of the Roman Empire). The party next to us lined up three corks on the table, which was also cluttered with highball glasses, before opening a fourth bottle when they got around to ordering dinner at 9:30. "Expense accounts," my companion concluded, wagging his finger at table after table. Other People's Money is not just an advisable safety net for all who enter here, but it's also obviously the unspoken foundation of the operation. Anyone without the imagination to run up an expense account need only wait for the next visit of the staff, which will anticipate and voice your most expensive desire before it has even crossed your mind.

Overestimating our needs (and credit limit), our waiter proposed not just any old after-dinner drink, but Remy Martin, and a cigar. We declined. He focused his gaze on my companion, who begged off the manly opportunity with the explanation that he wouldn't smoke one in front of me. "You could always take it with you and smoke it later," the waiter shot back. We held the trump card: No.

Coffee and dessert we did accept, however. Before bringing the bill (which came in around $150), he posed a final question. "Is there anything else I can do for you?" "Yes," I thought. "Tell me whether anyone has had a heart attack in here yet." People were ordering and drinking and eating and smoking as if there's no tomorrow. Given the nature of what they were consuming, there may not be.

Ladies' Fetish & Taboo Society
Compendium of Urban Anthropology, 1996

"The C student starts a restaurant. The A student writes restaurant reviews."

— P.J. O'ROURKE

EATING OUT IS FUN!
(HA!)

This essay contains full-throttle venting over a few incidents that were edited into submission in "When Service Goes To The Dogs."

When I was a child — long before theme park restaurants and fast food chains perverted our national taste buds — a trade association in Texas placed an instructive slogan in the margins of the ubiquitous combination kiddy menu and placemat that was routinely offered as sacrifice to post-toddler passions. As if it were not proof enough that Mom had been freed from the kitchen (and we, her captives, freed from the house), the menus excitedly reminded us of the true nature of what we were experiencing: Eating out is fun!

To me it was stating the obvious; any development that placed crayons in my hand was the very definition of fun, especially if the tactic didn't turn out to be a cover for some abomination like a shot or the dentist's drill. I knew eating out held the prospect of a grand time and maybe, if we were lucky, if the gods were favorably disposed, if we were at a cafeteria, dessert. My siblings, all younger, generally shared my viewpoint (particularly my brother, who, as if preparing for hibernation, stuffed himself to the point of pain on every family visit to the neighborhood Luby's, a memory with such profound staying power that 15 years later he refused to get out of the car when he saw that the cafeteria we'd driven to had changed to that name). If any of this was ever fun to my father, on the other hand, he didn't let on. He radiated a combination of annoyance and discomfort that peaked when the bill arrived and gave hint to the existence of darker currents in this business of eating out.

I now end up in restaurants with a frequency that should be considered decadent, but is probably just under the norm for not-quite-so-young urban professionals. A consequence is that the regularity of its occurrence long ago stripped eating out of any trace of being a special event. Still, I have not completely capitulated to mere utilitarianism. That childhood phrase still lurks within my psyche and regularly leaves its imprint on my expectations. I'm hoping to be more than fed when I go to a restaurant. I'm looking to be nourished, to be amused at least, entertained at best, and, if I'm lucky, to be so surprised and delighted that I want to stomp my feet or pound my hand on the table.[42]

The law of averages favors my quest, at least in the first two particulars, and serendipity occasionally comes through with the third. Unfortunately, those darker undercurrents, once hinted at by my father's behavior, have increasingly interjected themselves as well. More often than not, they color the experience as pervasively as I once did the kiddy menu. What triggers my discomfort is not picking up the tab, but what's heaped upon me before it arrives.

I do walk into restaurants with some knowledge of what it takes to run

them. A five-month stint as a tip slave taught me enough for a lifetime. At the end of college, despite my bookworm demeanor, I got a job as a cocktail waitress on the upper Greenville Avenue singles strip in North Dallas. The time and place were both ground zero for Happy Hour; it was the height

[42] It's been known to happen.

of the 1970s, when two-for-one drink prices were years away from state prohibition, and I was working in party animal central, the very place that pioneered frozen margaritas. (The owner invented the machine that made them.) I had the idea that the job would be relatively easy and the money good. I was wrong about both.

The first day alone was a crash course in the unrelenting tension and frustration that pervade food service. I walked into the kitchen and saw a waitress hurl a tray across the kitchen at a waiter and unleash a blood-curdling torrent of swearing. "What in the world would make somebody do that?" I wondered.

Lots of things, I soon learned. Nothing ever pushed me to such a satisfying, self-indulgent display as that waitress, who I'm pretty sure quit that day, but within a month, I was telling a manager I would throw up if he didn't get a chile relleno he wanted me to taste out of my face. I could cope with pranks;[43]

---

[43] Hell, I could pull 'em off with the best of them, and some of my co-workers were aces of stupidity, who'd turned the restaurant into a playground for our personal amusement. My specialty was bringing reading material that freaked out one of the managers. After he was startled to see me reading a German book during a day shift (not because I was reading, which I was allowed to do when no one was in the cantina, but because it was a foreign language other than Spanish), I made a point to throw him off balance. A Russian primer did it best. "My God – that's Outer Mongolian!" he shrieked.

In the universal bag of tricks, though, tortillas were an especially versatile tool. We'd roll them into cylinders, stick toothpicks through jalapeno slices, two on each end, to suggest wheels, and run the makeshift racing cars across tables before customers were seated. Or we'd cut them into Xs and Os and play tic-tac-toe on top of the crosshatched designs that had been conveniently laid onto the tabletops (again, before customers were there). We once managed to slip a tortilla prank into customer-occupied territory: In the safety of the kitchen we cut a smiley face out of a tortilla, rolled a wad of foil into a hook, and hung the face on the back of an unsuspecting waiter's apron as he was headed out into the dining room. The fact that we laughed ourselves into dribbling, quivering incoherence over that one is probably as much a commentary on the level of tension we endured as it is on the level of our maturity.

But the best and most ongoing prank of all was one that we had to live through straight-faced. The menu had a special group dinner, called, in an unintentional stroke of ironic genius, the *Revolucion* platter, that inevitably got ordered by packs of old Anglo ladies. The way this was served played up the celebration aspect: every waiter in the place had to pitch in, don a sombrero, and sing while loading platters on the table. And what they were to sing was "La Cucaracha," that catchy tune about the hard-to-catch varmint we call a cockroach. (Or maybe…something else.) As if there were not enough amusement value in serenading affluent blue hairs about an insect associated with filth while serving something named after a bloody break from tyranny, the waiters invariably went one step further. They rewrote the words (which were in Spanish, of course), to slip in descriptions of sexual acts upon their customers' female ancestors. The old women always beamed.

I could brush off the Cat Stevens lookalike Pakistani bartender biting my shoulder while I was hoisting a tray of double-your-pleasure margaritas for take-off; I could even deflect come-ons with split-second timing, not to mention enough wit to leave the refused favorable disposed toward the critical matter of the tip.

What was tricky – and the source of constant aggravation – was being first in the line of the customers' fire. I always owned up to my own flubs, and got adept at projecting "We'll pay for the dry cleaning!" over my shoulder while dashing back to the kitchen for a towel to wipe up a drink I'd spilled on a customer. Spills I got down to about one a week. Almost every shift, though, I had to take the heat for someone else's actions – a waiter in the restaurant bungling a drink order[44] (Me: You didn't order a Cutty and Coke? Repulsed customer: No, I said *Bacardi* and …), a waitress swiping what was rightfully my order of nachos, and customers trying to hold me responsible for what they had ordered. College students and high school counselors especially suffered a memory loss, on arrival of the bill, that subtracted a couple of rounds from the number I'd rung up and, inevitably, delivered. As far as management was concerned, collections were my problem; one way or another, the register amounts were coming out of my till at the end of the shift. I may have run out to the parking lot after a person who'd walked a bill, but no matter how badly I wanted to smash my tray onto someone's head, I never lost respect for the fact that the customer's wallet held the ultimate trump card.

This is a concept with astonishingly little currency in my recent experience

---

[44] Waitresses were allowed strangely limited duties in this place. We could not ascend to the better-paid status of bartender, because, we were told, we were not strong enough to pour the mix into the margarita machines. In the dining room we could only carry drinks to the table; the waiters took all orders, food and beverage, and collected all tabs. We had free and sole reign over the cantina, though, the terrain of college students and divorcees and altogether too many people asking whether Trini Lopez, a decade after singing about what he'd do with a hammer, was going to sit in with the band that night. (He never did.) Guess where the tips were better.

on the other end of restaurant transactions. Now, adult life (more particularly, working with law firms) long ago taught me that common decency is not sufficient reason for some people to treat their fellow mortals as human beings. Neither, for some people, is furthering one's economic self-interest. At least, not for a troubling number of servers I've encountered lately – who've responded in ways that can be charitably described as self-sabotage, to provocation no greater than a customer's merely existing.

The first happened when I was in the company of veteran business luncher and unfailingly polite person James Willia Griffith,[45] who has an unsurpassed flair for playing up to people in the service industry. We'd decided to try Palace Cafe, which had recently opened in the ground floor of the Hogg Palace,[46] an architecturally colored building in downtown Houston that's been converted into apartments. One step in the door was enough to trigger doubts about the comfort level within. The Cafe traffics in post-modern industrial chic, with exposed duct work, rough walls sponged a weird amalgam of mustard and gold, and nary a surface to cushion the ambient noise (not to mention nary a notion to modulate across-the-board over-amplified CDs).

Being ushered to a chair that had been pre-littered with mashed potatoes

---

[45] The typo in his middle name is historic. It occurred repeatedly in our high school newspaper's galleys for the honor roll. The Linotype machine initially spewed out a total number of characters per name that happened to be one fewer than Bill's had. We staffers were always having to put back the final "m" in his middle name. When I moved to Houston, it was to a neighborhood with a street named Willia. Which intersects with a street bearing the name of our high school choir director.

[46] I don't care what you've heard: Ima Hogg did *not* have a sister named Ura.

for our convenience did not improve the impression. Nor did the unexpected extra alongside the table: Bill rested his arm on the window sill and lifted a shirt sleeve dusted with ashes. We inspected our surroundings suspiciously while waiting for the waitress to find us. The chairs, which were easily 30 years old in style and color, overstuffed semi-circled, burnt orange and electric green that fit awkwardly against the low, tiny tables, did not fare well under our scrutiny, which fixated on armrests worn dingy with we didn't want to know what. Nor was the floor a welcome sight; it had been stripped to a most unappetizing base.

Bill was still clearing away his personal space when the waitress joined us. She intimated that something was amiss with him.

"His chair's got mashed potatoes on it," I said. She ignored me.

"Look at this," Bill said, lifting an ash-covered sleeve. "The window sill's covered with ashes."

"There can't be ashes," she said."There's no smoking here."

Bill put his arm down on the sill again and lifted it to show her evidence to the contrary.

We pause now for a pop quiz. Her response was:

> (a) to say, "I'm sorry;"
>
> (b) to offer a towel;
>
> (c) to wipe his shirt sleeve;
>
> (d) to wipe the window sill;
>
> (e) any combination of a-d.

It was a trick question. The answer wasn't on the quiz! It was (f) to blame the customer. What she said was along the lines of "Oh, that's smart, putting your arm back in it." Whereupon she asked for our order. Give us a clean table, we should have said. And while you're at it, throw in a copy of Dale Carnegie's bestseller for yourself. It'd give you something to do when you're not waiting on customers.

The same book would have made an appropriate tip for the staff at Bayou City Oyster Company last December, where an insouciant response got the attention of more than one table. My booth had six people, five of us digging into a platter of crawfish and one preferring to drink his dinner. The reason for his choice formed the topic of our conversation. He'd had an uncommonly awful day at his job, which is in a service industry; the folks in the main office had not done what the customer had paid for, and he'd been the fan everything hit. His misery became complete when he saw something floating in the Scotch he'd been drinking. The something turned out to be a bug.

Call the waitress over and tell her, I suggested; maybe this was a chance for his day to improve. Maybe she'd comp it or give him another for free. Maybe I should have kept my big mouth shut.

One who reserves obnoxiousness for close friends, Rick passed on the new cautiously and gently. The waitress took in this new development without flinching, and certainly without apologizing. She returned with a message. "The bartender says he's not going to open a new bottle," she said.

"I want a bug in my drink," a man announced from a neighboring table. She walked off.

The turn of events caused the Scotch-and-bug drinker to ponder his relationship with the restaurant's owner, for whom he'd made signs in a previous career, (His handiwork, which he pointed out, was a mudbug on a wall behind us.) "He's good in the food-making department," Rick said. "Good in the signage department. Bad in the bugs-in-drinks department."

The drink was on the bill.

Both these waitresses must bow before their masters, though, who staff a well-regarded, ever-so-popular Montrose eatery by the name of Ruggles Bar and Grill, which is a standing testimony that it is indeed possible to get too much of a good thing. My most recent meal there (and it may well be my last) was easily the most extreme of my life: terrific food in a relentlessly repelling environment.

My companion in this unintended flagellation was my pal Ben, who is an amiable, easy-going sort, prone to a charming graciousness when dealing with anyone who might possibly bring him food. Happy to wait at the bar, we arrived 30 minutes early for our reservations. Though the restaurant had been open for only 10 minutes (assuming that its stated hours bear any honest relationship to reality), most of the tables in both dining rooms were filled and people were already clogging the narrow reception area. (This was before 6 p.m. on a Sunday, not a time previously associated, in my experience, with high restaurant demand.) Nonetheless, the receptionist said she could seat us immediately. It was the only pleasant surprise of the experience.

We got the table from hell. It was in a sunken porch that did multiple duty as bar, dining room, and holding tank for customers waiting for tables. It was at the foot of the stairs used by every single person who walked into the room (or, in the case of the waiters, in and out and in and out). It was directly in the line of fire of waiters dashing to and from the bar, most of whom allowed us only inches clearance, and many of whom knocked the unoccupied chair into the table and, below that, into my knees. It was directly in the line of sight of mushrooming hordes of would-be diners, who spilled from the narrow reception area into the apparently more enticing, certainly more spacious bar, where they took rest, hovering closer and closer to us.

Our waiter only worsened the sense of being hounded, harried, and outright battered. He hurried us at every step of the way, and more fools we for not having welcomed it. He didn't light up at the universal signal for "We're Going to Spend Money," ordering an appetizer, and it took another course for us to realize that he was more interested in turning the table than the size of our tab. A bus boy who did not embrace the waiter's attitude made the first attempt to deliver salads. He aborted his mission after a long-distance sighting of the state of our tabletop, which was crowded by crockery as oversized as props for an Edith Ann skit. Within two minutes, the salads returned in the clutches of our more determined waiter, who made it clear that delaying the greens any longer was not an option. He whisked away the appetizer and side plates (which still contained food, and not just niggardly morsels) without asking if we were through, which we were not. Before we had time to protest, he'd switched the plates and walked away, while we sat slack-jawed over another set of ridiculous plates that engulfed our table.

By the entree, Ben had spiraled into an animal-instinct irritability, triggered by a relentless stream of people passing within inches of his arm. A throbbing in my throat made me realize we were shouting to be heard about the combined din of synthesizer music, ambient chatter, and intermittent squealing from a neighboring party of what appeared to be dancers. A memory of my last visit flashed through my brain: One of my companions had stood up and drunkenly proclaimed her love for me, in a universal, non-sexual, but definitely high decibel way. Maybe it hadn't been an aberration that no one had noticed the outburst.

Obviously gluttons for more than the food, Ben and I ordered dessert and coffee. The waiter delivered the check with the desserts, which were on plates as humongous as their predecessors. Coffee arrived not far behind, in a manner that pushed the affair over the brink it'd been tottering on and into the unsalvageably absurd. The cups were not on saucers, but on platters easily nine inches long. The non-coffee-cup portions of the platters were filled with napkins, on top of which rested a delicate and, dare I say, small cookie. Logistics resulted in my cup and platter being planted along the opposite side of the table. Every sip of coffee required a commute as predicate. Fortunately, the inconvenience was brief. Ben's last sip of coffee drew the waiter like a magnet. He didn't offer refills, even though we were still working on our desserts – he cleared away Ben's coffee platter, even though it held a cookie that was clearly still in the process of being eaten.

The consequences of their own cluelessness coming down on places like this trio of offenders is, unfortunately, usually only the stuff of fantasy. Ruggles has received a bit of a beating in the press of late; the *Houston Chronicle*'s "Whining & Dining" column has printed several readers' complaints of treatment far worse than mine, including being advised, on seating, that a table had a one-hour limit, which the owners promptly denied in print. Recently, though, I stumbled onto a dream come true. I got to do more than just gloat over the morning paper; I got to watch the awakening of one new restaurant to the terrifying extent of its blundering, which had begun even before opening.

The name of the place alone cried out three-alarm misguidedness. Yet even as much as it's begging for ridicule to launch a business under the name Fakawwee Lodge ("Fakaw-you, fakaw-me, fakaw-wheeeee" – or, as my friend Rex put it, "fakaw-all-of-us" – now here's a business plan that might be worth reading), the moniker across this new Houston restaurant is still a wiser choice than what was originally announced: Karankawa Lodge. The Karankawas, besides being among the Gulf Coast's original inhabitants, were known for two traits in particular: They reputedly smelled to high heaven, from smearing themselves with fish to ward off mosquitoes (and other predators). They were also said – though this characteristic has been disproven – to be cannibals.

Ben and I walked into the place a day after it had been condemned to a speedy death by a review in the *Houston Press*. It was a rare case of being in a weird place at the right time. As a result, we were the beneficiaries of a spin control that reached desperate – and highly entertaining – proportions.

The chosen name does fit, in a strange way; the décor is so disjoint and bizarre that it raises questions along the lines of "Where the Fakawwee?" The mishmash of trophy heads (sailfish – *sailfish?* – with mountain sheep and bears) and artifacts are not consistent with any one geographic region; the coexistence of Hopi kachinas and a totem pole particularly creates a United Nations "We Are Family" air.

A quick perusal of the menu prompted Ben to warn, "Be veh-wy quiwet." The menu offered the chance to devour most of Warner Brothers' stable of cartoon characters, except with wild boar instead of the Tasmanian Devil. There was even a set of antlers nearby, mounted on something resembling Elmer Fudd's magic helmet. Everything held fodder for hysterical laughter. Fortunately, the restaurant also provided a cover for our outbursts: a 60s and 70s cover band playing so loudly in the lounge that Rex heard them through closed car windows when he drove by that night.

Of course we would be in a place this absurd that I would encounter the most obsequious, solicitous server of my life. The waiter welcomed us to the "Fa-KAH-wee" and recited the chef's credentials and awards. He brought me a beer sample, characterized the Lodge as having Nietzschean layers of reality, and used the phase "one-point perspective" to describe a planned mural. One manager decked out in a mini-suit and gold jewelry after another came by the table to ask if the band was bothering us and whether we would like the volume turned down. Being asked was amazing by itself; being listened to was even more so.

At the second break, someone turned on music that made me long for the band, at any volume – a song by Barry White. When it finished, I shut my eyes and concentrated on the next song being by anyone other than Barry White. I was spectacularly unsuccessful. Next up was the Barry White Song That Would Not End. For the remainder of the break – 20 minutes easily – it moaned and sighed and groaned, till it hit a loop of fading out as if at an end, only to fade back in moments later, suffer an orchestrated hiccup and give way to Barry's crooning, "I have sooooooooooooo much to give."

It was a relief when the band returned, having broken and been glued back together, as Ben put it. While they launched into a medley of Fabulous

Thunderbirds hits, beginning with the anti-littering jingle "Don't Mess With Texas," Barry's unwelcome tones crept back in. "I've got sooooooo much to give," he sang. "Am I tuff enough?" sang the band. "I've got sooooooo much to give," Barry countered. The interplay reduced me to howling, to wheezing, to tears, to resting my head on folded arms and gasping for breath.[47] The waiter, who was clearing the table, discreetly took no note of the quivering mass that had been his customer. As soon as Ben called the man's attention to the aural layering, he promptly cut Barry off. When my breathing returned to normal, an explanation for the song fell into my head: Instead of a dance mix, we'd been treated to an extended fuck mix.

"Please come back. You'll come back, won't you?" begged the waiter. As did the blonde manager who came by the table. And the brunette manager folding napkins at the edge of the dining room. And the black-haired manager in the door, who followed us out to the sidewalk.

I just might. For a change, eating out really was fun.

Ladies' Fetish & Taboo Society
Compendium of Urban Anthropology, 1998

---

[47] The last time I laughed this hard in a restaurant, big-haired women in stiletto heels were touch-dancing to Soviet emigrés singing Russian pop and weirdly accented Joe Cocker and Tom Jones tunes to a karaoke machine amidst helium balloons bearing images of sunflowers and get-well wishes, in a dining room with whorehouse red walls stenciled with gold fleur-de-lis, steel-green drapes fit for Carol Burnett's Scarlett O'Hara, and tiger-print upholstery. "I feel like we're in a Matt Helm movie!" my companion howled. We plummeted over the edge when dessert arrived and his ice cream was crowned with berries on a stick. "I've never had ice cream with an antenna before!" (The Stoli Grill; far west Houston; go!)

ACKNOWLEDGMENTS

Thank you to Kevin Dubose and Doug Miller for unwittingly setting me on this path. I owe undying gratitude to Rex Gillit, Bill Griffith, and Ben Hadad for serving as witnesses to and sounding boards for my adventures. Rex deserves special mention for enduring so many dreadful bars, labeling the phenomenon of the "omni-directional Scud lust missile," and serving for decades beyond any call as my personal Capricorn/life commentator.

Most writers are lucky to encounter one simpatico editor; I was blessed with two, Teresa Byrne-Dodge and Lisa Gray, both uncommonly supportive and respectful and who indulged my pursuit of whims. I am grateful to the indomitable Maria Moss for opening the door to taking over her column at *Diversion*, and to Sabrina Pacifici, publisher of *LLRX.com*, for welcoming freewheeling pursuit of leads that came across my meandering path.

I am indebted to John-Michael Albert, Trav S.D., Sue Reddel, and Kihm Winship for reading and commenting on the collection in progress. Noah Diamond and Kelley Loftus shared keen eyes and generous notes on it beyond the call of friendship. Zoë Biehl provided thorough and insightful copyediting, as well as a millennial, multicultural perspective that led to deleting or reshaping a couple of sections that come across differently now than what I consciously intended when I wrote them years ago. Matthew Foster deployed his skill for translating my vague descriptions into visual design and produced a front cover graphic that delightfully matched the image in my head. I am also grateful to Suzanne Savoy for a photo that gives fair warning of the attitude that awaits within these pages. Noah Diamond gets seconds in the thanks department for gracing my words with a well-considered, witty book design, beyond my wildest hopes.

I owe all y'all a drink or three.

ABOUT THE AUTHOR

Kathy Biehl once tested a pal's potential boyfriend with a cut-glass party platter of circus peanuts, Little Debbie Snack Cakes, Snoballs, Twinkies, and Hostess Cupcakes. (He flunked.) She has spent some 30 years being paid to eat, drink, and type up her observations. For more than a decade she reviewed restaurants for *The Houston Business Journal, Houston Press, Time Out New York* (including its first dining guide), and a slew of online directories and guides. She also contributed cover stories to Houston's dining magazine *My Table* and wrote the food news column for the doctor's travel and leisure magazine *Diversion* and the legal research journal *LLRX.com*. She is the editrix and primary writer of the zine *Ladies' Fetish & Taboo Society Compendium of Urban Anthropology* and its companion blogs. Her food writing has won awards from the Association of Food Journalists and Houston Press Club, as well as the title Pseudo-Food XPert, from a review subject she'd caught impersonating a competitor.

Her food adventures now explore a largely plant-based diet. She keeps her computer and spreadsheets out of the kitchen.

CPSIA information can be obtained
at www.ICGtesting.com
Printed in the USA
BVHW071827270421
605952BV00011B/702